Information Process and Retrieval

C.K. Sharma
(Ex-Chief Librarian and Reader/Chairman
Dr. B.R. Ambedkar University, Agra)
Reader/Chairman, Library & Information Science Department
M.M. Modi (P.G.) College, Modinagar

A.K. Sharma
Librarian
Shyam Lal College (Eve.)
University of Delhi, Delhi

ATLANTIC
PUBLISHERS & DISTRIBUTORS (P) LTD

Published by

ATLANTIC

PUBLISHERS & DISTRIBUTORS (P) LTD

7/22, Ansari Road, Darya Ganj, New Delhi-110002
Phones : +91-11-40775252, 40775214, 23273880, 23275880
Fax: +91-11-23285873
Web: www.atlanticbooks.com
E-mail: orders@atlanticbooks.com

Disclaimer

- The author and the publisher have taken every effort to the maximum of their skill, expertise and knowledge to provide correct material in the book. Even then if some mistakes persist in the content of the book, the publisher does not take responsibility for the same. The publisher shall have no liability to any person or entity with respect to any loss or damage caused, or alleged to have been caused directly or indirectly, by the information contained in this book.
- The author has fully tried to follow the copyright law. However, if any work is found to be similar, it is unintentional and the same should not be used as defamatory or to file legal suit against the author.
- If the readers find any mistakes, we shall be grateful to them for pointing out those to us so that these can be corrected in the next edition.
- All disputes are subject to the jurisdiction of Delhi courts only.

Printed & bound in India by Atlantic Print Services

Preface

There is now broad consensus that Information Technology, being a driving force in global economy, is shaping our world. Information technology requires of the knowledge of self-managed learning, scientific and technological terms, information handling, selection, retrieval and critical assessment of information, system design, inquiry exploration and experimentation. An in-depth study of the present book will enable the readers to have at least little acquaintance with this technology. It is a complete treatise on information process that includes indexing, abstracting, citation indexing, bibliometrics, webomterics, and Greenhouse software. It also focuses on information retrieval, which is a communication process that links the information user to a librarian. The communication normally involves the processing of text.

The book is primarily about computer-based retrieval systems and its purpose is to teach how the retrieval systems work. Needless to mention, it will prove extremely useful to all computer users in general and those concerned with libraries and library science in particular.

I take this opportunity to acknowledge all my colleagues as well as students who encouraged and supported me in completing this great task. I will always remain thankful to them.

C.K. SHARMA

Contents

Index/Indexing

1

The term 'Index' is derived from the Latin word 'indicare' which means to indicate or to point out. In other words an index is a systematic list of items contained in the document or article. It works as a guide to the reader to trace his document or information contained in other primary sources.

It is represented by entries arranged alphabetically or in a subject-wise or classified manner.

Encyclopedia of Lib. Sc.

Index is a device that serves as a pointer or an indicator, more often an alphabetical list that includes subjects and names of the persons which have significance in graphic record. Chakraverty in his book *Indexing Principles: Process and Products* defined index as "a systematic guide to the items of a collection or the concepts derived from it. It comprises entries arranged in known or searchable order with reference to show where each item indexed is located".

BSI (3700-1954)

An index consists of series of entries appearing not in the order in which they appear in the publication but in some other order (e.g. alphabetical) chosen to enable the user to find them quickly together with the references to show where each item is located.

However, Index is a systematic list of documents or items published which guides the reader to locate or to retrieve the required items. Generally it is arranged alphabetically.

In view of the above definitions, index may be defined as:

"It is a guide to the names, items, concepts and places given in the document or articles arranged systematically, preferably in an alphabetical order. It also contains references to locate the document".

1.1 Functions of an Index

Index is a reference tool to help the user to retrieve information of a document since the published literature has been growing rapidly and information of the literature is very important for research and decision-making. It has increased the use of index. It performs the following functions:

(a) Index provides guidance to the user regarding material, its search and retrieval.

(b) It guides the user regarding the name of the authors.

(c) It guides the user about documents by subject.

(d) It saves the time of the user.

(e) Index provides bibliographical details of the documents.

(f) It provides reference guides which help the reader to locate the document.

(g) Terminology and spellings are provided by the Index.

(h) It help researchers, scientists to select their documents.

1.2 Development of Index

In ancient period, the manuscripts were arranged by size, colour and binding. The term index was used to denote the list or a 'catalogue' or a 'title' of a document. The first step was the tag of the parchament which was tied up to a papyrus roll for its identification. During the Greek period, the scholars of Alexanderia used the symbols to indicate particular information in the text. At a later period, the walls and pillars of the temples, viharas and mosques were used to write the names of the writer, title of the MSS in unsystematic manner. During the Muslim period and the advent of the printing press, manuscripts were produced and arranged and their contents were written on the front page of the document which was generally alphabetically arranged.

During the 17th century, the classics or scholarly books had index in it. The indexes of 'History of Great Britannica' by Speed (1611) and the 'Acts and Ordinances of Parliament' by Scobell (1956) are important. There are a few periodicals which had indexes, e.g. Acta Erudicterum. During the 18th century professional indexers emerged. In 1737, Alexander Cruden published the "Concordance to the Bible", indexing the Bible. It was a significant work and was appreciated. Other works of this period were:

1. Johnson's "Dictionary of the English Language" (1755).
2. Johnson's "General Index both of Maxims and Reflexions" (1759).

By the time there was tremendous improvement in indexing. People knew the importance of the index which makes the index more popular. The other important improvement was the step taken by the *Encyclopedia Britannica* which published its index as a separate volume. It was followed by the *Chamber's Encyclopedia* in 1874.

The real improvement came when William Frederick Poole brought out "Index to Periodical Literature" 1801-1906. It was the first index in the history of periodical indexing, covering articles and creating subject entries from the keywords in the titles of the articles indexed. Poole also took this work to the societies and the professionals, which resulted in the formation of societies called 'Index Society". This society took the indexing work speedily and published many indexes.

During the 20th century the indexing work was taken as an important work to provide document to the users. H.W. Wilson brought out the "Reader's Guide to Periodical Literature". It was the first indexing service of its type providing subject access to the current micro-documents. This followed many indexes like: 'Applied Science and Technology Index', 'British Technology Index', 'Education Index', 'Guide to Indian Periodical Index', 'Index Medicus', 'Index India', 'Indian Science Index', 'Science Citation Index', and 'Social Science Index', etc.

1.3 Types of Indexes

There are many types of indexes:

1. Alphabetico-specific index

2. Alphabetico-classed Index
3. Author Index
4. Cumulative Index
5. Classified Index
6. Chain Index
7. PRECIS
8. POPSI
9. Citation Index
10. Coordinate Index (Pre-coordinate and Post-coordinate Index)
11. Computer-based Index
    (a) KWIC
    (b) KWOC

1.3.1 Alphabetico-specific index

In this index, index entries are made directly under the name of the subject. Headings represent more or less the subject which is of specific nature. The subject is related to the subject of the items being indexed. In other words subject entries are made and filled under subject words in normal and natural language sequence. The items described in subject are represented by the terms.

Example: Dog
Explanatory subjects—Zoology, Domestic animal and dog
Entry element (Term)—DOG

But the specific subject is related to other subjects also like Zoology—Domestic animal or because it is (DOG) an integral part of the Extension subjects. The specific subject (DOG) is linked up with the general and coordinated subjects by making the use of 'see also' references—'see' references may be used if required.

Under the Alphabetico-specific index, the most specific term is selected as the heading of the document.

Example: Introdution of *DOG* (Term)
Behaviour of *DOG* (Term)

Similarly a document on SUN will have the subject heading SUN (Not SOLAR SYSTEM) or 'Astronomy'.

Merits

(a) Indexer's choice. An indexer does not need a complete and all subject headings. He can select his own subject which is appropriate for the index and is suitable to users.

(b) Independent subject headings—Generally classification schemes are followed for subject headings. But if any subject heading given in the classification scheme is not appropriate, it can be avoided.

(c) There should be promptness as the distinctive feature of specific subject as it retrieves the information.

1.3.2 Drawbacks

(a) Independent subject headings are based on indexer's choice, which may tend to separate related classes and subject. They are used in index on account of their various treatments.

Example: Engineer
Mechanical Engineer
Chemical Engineer
Electrical Engineer

(b) Specific subjects are used in index, but there are other related subjects which can be included or used in index by using "see also" reference entries, which makes more entries unnecessary.

(c) Reference entries are generally inconsistent, unreliable and complex. This fault can lead to lack of faith in the index.

1.3.3 Alphabetico-classed index

The headings used in Alphabetico-classed index are entry words which are classed term-specific terms which are used for specific subject of the document. Specific topics are preferred.

Example: Aluminium (specific topic)
Other generic terms—Chemistry, Inorganic, Metallic documents.

Specific topics are grouped and filed alphabetically. In this index, all terms—specific and general—are included in the index. There is hardly any reference entry used. The arrangement of the index heading under a broad subject makes it a more suitable index for searching the generic subjects.

1.3.4 Author index

These indexes have author approach. Author may be a personal or corporate author. The Index may be a Personal Author Index, or Corporate Author Index. Author Index may cover the personal and corporate names in alphabetical sequence. Author Index provides entry for main author and other subsequent or collaborator authors.

Example: Pawar, Ramesh H.1. 2103
Prevendra 1.273
Pitambar H.A. 1131
Prem Chand P.S. 2112
Pushkar 3431
Sharma, Amit
Academic libraries 2719
Prison Libraries 3510
Union Catalogue 1309
Singh, Sukhvir
Catalogue of Serials 2173
Classification Scheme 2431

1.3.5 Subject index

Subject approach may be catered for by such indexes as subject index. It is also known as keyword index as keywords represent the subject. There may be many subject indexes, i.e.

(a) Keyword index
(b) Formula index
(c) Ring Index
(d) Locality index
(e) Taxonomic Index

Example: Common Subject Index

1.3.6 Document index

It has a document approach, i.e. Patent Index, Numerical Patent Index, Concordance, Translation Index, Report Index, Conference Index, Book Index, Bibliography Index.

In other form or covering other aspects it may be Contract Number Index, Accession Number Index, Patent Number Index, Report Number Index, Registry Number Index.

1.3.7 Cumulative index

A cumulative index, covering a number of volumes, is generally issued as a separate volume.

Example: Cumulative index to Indian Journals of Genetics and Plant Breeding. Vol. 1-33; 1941-78. By R.G. Prasar.

1.4 Classified Indexing

Classified index or the subject classification with its techniques helps in literature searching system or information retrieval device. It is distinguished from the subject headings and alphabetical index. A classified index uses figures or letter symbols, arranged in the order of the symbols and notations. This is a logical sequence bringing related subjects together. Words are not used in the indexing and alphabetization is also not followed. In other words it may be mentioned that classified indexing is arranged according to notations or arranged in notational order which is according to classification scheme.

In classified indexing:

1. Entries are filed in notational order.
2. Classification scheme is followed.
3. Sequence is kept according to classification schemes.
4. Classified subject index will follow the classified indexing.

5. It groups related topics which begin with general topics to specific topics.
6. Specific topic is included in general topic.

In classified indexing, the hierarchy is maintained among the topics. Topics have their position predetermined.

Merits

1. It beings all related topics together.
2. It avoids cross reference entries.
3. There are less chances of synonyms and homonyms.
4. Classification notations deal with the concept but not the titles.
5. It can be recognized as global system and may be accepted by all countries.

Demerits

1. Coordinate search is difficult to conduct.
2. Specific search is somewhat hard to conduct.
3. Classification scheme is not known to users.
4. Classified file of subject entries are to be converted into alphabetical arrangement of subjects, author and title.
5. Indexing is limited to classification scheme.
6. It has an arbitrary structure of the system.

The classified indexing can be a more efficient system if:

1. Freely faceted scheme of classification is followed.
2. Feature heading are derived according to a Postulate Based Subject Indexing such as Chain Indexing and POPSI.

1.4.1. Special features of classified indexing

1. Entries of document may be arranged of:
   (a) Compound subjects with basic subjects.
   (b) Compound subjects with one and the same basic subjects.
   (c) Components of a compound subject with basic subject.

2. Subject arrangement is consistently maintained.
3. Search of document is made among the entries.

1.4.2 Bibliographic index

The index of the literature of a particular subject, consisting of micro-documents, is called subject index or Bibliographical Index. It consists of subject headings to an item so that its subject contents are revealed.

1.4.3 Ranganathan's relative index

Ranganathan used certain abbreviations to indicate various contents. He used devices of inversion, punctuation, indentation to provide the context:

Note:

1. The Index Number is the number of the part, chapter, or section of the occurrence of the item indexed.
2. For example, the index number MH 7 means Sec. 7 of Chap. MH in Part M.
3. The following abbreviations are used:

def = Definition
desc = Described
irt = in relation to
qirt = Quoted in relation to
rirt = Referred in relation to

Bengali Surname	PB2
Bibliographical entries	BC4
Bi-partite catalogue	BD42
Boarding classes	AC3
Canon of	
Ascertainability irt	
Uniformity in catalogue	PC5
Variations in practice	BC6
Consistence	MH6
Permanence	MB1
Prepotence	MA

Card

Catalogue	BE
Technique	BE3
Catalogue Choice of	MP1
Code	BG

Source: S.R. Ranganathan, Cataloguing Practice, 2nd. ed. Bombay: Asia, 1974.

1.5 Coordinate Indexing

Coordinate indexing is one of the most exciting techniques of information retrieval of coordinating concepts. It is a combination rather than permutation. In fact, all the alphabetical indexing methods are coordinate index systems. They are coordination methods. They coordinate two or more concepts represented by the terms individually or in some other combinations. If combination is not followed, the contents representation of the documents shall neither be specific nor accurate. M. Tauba introduced Uniterm system in 1951. It is multidimensional indexing system which is also known as alphabetical subject approach. It helps in information retrieval.

Uniterm is a class label consisting of single word. A document is to be indexed into the uniterm system by describing its subject content in terms of single-word labels. Class labels (uniterm) are used in the document text or the single word selected by an indexer to describe subject contents. There is a knowledge proliferation and the material has created a problem as to how to control it for its maximum utilization by the user. Index has somehow contributed to solve this problem. It is effective in retrieving the information.

Coordinate indexing has been categorised in two categories:

1. Pre-coordinate indexing
2. Post-coordinate indexing

1.5.1 Pre-coordinate indexing

Index terms are important in an index. They are combined and coordinated in many ways. The words which are used to make up the index headings are combined or coordinated while preparing indexing. These headings are points of indexing out of which suitable or access points among them are selected and used in an index. The selected headings or the access points are modified with a word, phrase (term) and forms a subject indexing. They follow an appropriate sequence which may suit the majority of the users. Kaiser, Coates, Ranganathan, Sharp, Austri and Farradane have made valuable contribution in evolving a sequence in such a way that these words, phrases may be coordinated at access point (input level) whilc building up the index file. This developed indexing system which was pre-coordinate indexing system.

Pre-coordinate indexing systems are mostly item-on-term systems. For example, alphabetical subject catalogue and classified catalogue. All these catalogues were made on card form of 5' × 3' which included bibliographical description of the single document and it was a unit record.

For example, Relative index of DDC and classified index of colon classification.

Special Features

1. Subject headings consist of two or many index terms.
2. The index terms are arranged in predetermined order (pre-coordinated)
3. There are multi access points for each document following a particular pattern of coordination.

Example

1. Chain indexing
2. PRECIS
3. POPSI

They are Pre-coordinate indexing systems because in these systems index terms are coordinated at access point (entry point). The process is given below:

1. Subject of document is analysed.
2. Constituent concepts are derived by analysis.
3. Concepts, then represented by symbols or words are used in indexing language.

4. These symbols or words are finally arranged in logical order.
5. The logical order follows the syntax of the indexing language to derive the subject formulative.
6. These pre-coordinated subject formulations are arranged in an order in the index file.
7. These subject headings are key to the contents of the document collection.

In view of the above, it may be concluded that in a pre-coordinate indexing system:

1. They are based on subject analysis of documents.
2. They follow some citation order of terms.
3. Coordination is done at the input stage.

Search in pre-coordinate indexing

In Pre-coordinate indexing the most important aspect is to determine the order of significance. Searching in index is simple. If a user wants to find out the available document on heart disease, he has to formulate the request in the form of the term which is relevant, without any notice to its citation order. The selected terms will be 'disease' and 'heart'. These entries in the index will be picked up one by one from their alphabetic position. It will be better to start with the term card which has the number of postings. Each posted number in the term card is compared one by one with another term card.

Limitations

There are some limitations of the pre-coordinate indexing:

1. A particular sequence of coordination of index term may not meet the approaches of all the users of index file.
2. Though multiple entry system may overcome the limitations, even this covers only a fraction of the possible number of total permutation. Thus, the index file may fail to provide a particular combination which a user may be looking for.

3. Indexers are not fully aware of the intricacies of the order of significance before starting their search.
4. This system requires intellectual involvement on the part of the indexer.
5. Pre-coordination of index terms may be too broad for a particular search.
6. The user has no freedom to manipulate the coordination of terms in a derived manner.

1.5.2 Post-coordinate indexing

In this system, the concepts representing a composit subject are kept separately uncoordinated by the indexer. The coordination of component concepts or index terms is done by the searcher at the search or output stage. Coordination of concepts could be done at the time of search. The indexing systems which are based on this basic principle are collectively called post-coordinate indexes. This index is usually called coordinate index, the words and phrases selected at the time of indexing can either be searched individually or be combined at the time of searching the index.

Characteristics

1. It is based on subject analysis.
2. No fixed citation order is maintained.
3. Coordination of index terms is done by the user of the output or search state.

There are four persons who have introduced their coordinate systems, e.g. W.E. Batten (UK), G. Cordonnier (France), Calvin Maoers (USA) and Mortimer Taube (USA). But the system developed by Taube is more popular.

Term Entry and Item Entry System

The post-coordinate system is of two types:

(a) Term entry

(b) Item entry system

Term entry system is that where term cards are posted with relevant document numbers.

Example: 1. Uniterm Method 2. Optical Coincidence method

Item Entry System is the system in which one card is maintained for a document. The relevant concept of subject matter of the document is represented in code form by a series of notches punched out from the holes along the margin of the card and the control area of the card is used for document description.

1.5.3 Difference between pre-coordinate & post-coordinate

1. Both indexing systems follow the process of concept coordinations—but it is in two different stages.
2. In pre-coordinate indexing, coordination of concept is done at the input stage while preparing the index. While in post-coordinate indexing system, the coordination of concept is done at the output stage.
3. Pre-coordinate is a system of non-manipulation while post-coordinate is a manipulative system because it permits a greater degree of search manipulation.
4. Both types of systems have the ability to coordinate or correlate classes, one at the time of indexing and the other while searching.
5. Pre-coordinate system is a system in which alphabetical subject catalogues and the conventional classified catalogue having class relationship are expressed once and for all before the indexing operation. But in post-coordinate system, class relations are manipulated or exploited by manipulation of classes at the time of searching.

1.6 Uniterm Indexing System

Uniterm means two terms or a combination of two words, units or terms. Unit stands for a single word. Uniterm means a single word representing a single concept. This index system is a post-coordinate indexing system based on term entry principle. Mortimer Taube introduced the Uniterm System in 1955.

It appears to be a simple system. It brings out characteristics and the logic of the post-coordinate system of indexing very clearly.

Index entries are to consist of unit terms as opposed to composit headings. Its process is as under:

1. Subject contents of document are analysed, like other systems.
2. Individual concept is isolated.
3. If five concept terms are isolated or if the subject of document is represented by five terms, then five separate entries or term cards are prepared. Though it will not be economical to post a full document description in all the entry cards an alternative has been devised.

   Instead of description, a unique identification number of document (i.e. Accession Number) is posted in each of the term cards. Any other unique number may also be posted instead.
4. For quick scanning of posted number in an entry, the card is divided into 10 columns—1 to 0 or 0—9. The terminal digit of a number determines the column of its posting. (No. 25, 465, 1175 will be posted in 5 columns).
5. Some space is left on the top of the card allotted for the term. Rest of the area is divided into ten columns.
6. The entries thus prepared are kept alphabetically arranged in a tray just like catalogue cards.
7. While more or more documents are collected, the term card has on it more and more number of documents.
8. Even for single document a term card is prepared.

TREATMENT							
21	12		44	45	55		510
	22						

- Accession Number

RETINE							
41	52 112 152	123	14 34 44			59	740

DISEASE									
31			24 44	125	6 56 156 276	77	58	19	30 140

The above is a set of 3-term card.

1.6.1 Searching

In this system, readymade subject headings are not provided for indexing. Every term is dependent on all other terms and serves as individual access point to all related items in the collection. Searching starts after the completion of indexing operation, there is a list of uniterms, from which the appropriate one is chosen to represent a document. If a document is multifocal or compound or complex, it may thus be represented by more than one uniterm.

Each uniterm is a unit of information for which a separate card is assigned.

Example: Document 134

"Fire Hazards connected elevators in library building"

Fire Hazards
Elevator
Library building] Three concepts

Each uniterm concept will have a separate or three individual entries in their respective alpbahetical positions. The Accession Number 134 will be put on all three cards assigned to uniconcepts in 6th column of the card.

The system is based on the principle that each title of the document can be reduced for indexing purpose to a number of basic ideas capable of being presented by uniterms. Thus, in this system readymade subject headings are not provided by the indexes.

1.6.2 Document identification number

Each document is given an identification number. This can be an accession number of the document. The accession file is maintained according to these accession numbers.

Document File

Sharma, C.K.

Modern Library Systems. Agra: Y.K.
Publisher, 1985.
437p.

2725

These entries are made on card and are called Document Profiles. In place of accession number a serial number may also be given to each card. It serves an identification number. Each card gives bibliographical details of the document it represents.

1.6.3 Search of uniterm

Uniterm is a single word for single concept. It is like a keyword taken from the document to be indexed. It represents the contents or the ideas and concepts of a document. Thus, uniterms are the units of information available in the document. Generally, one subject inherits more than one uniterm. Such documents are indexed under each uniterm.

Example: Classification and cataloguing in the libraries of India. It has four concepts:

(a) Classification
(b) Cataloguing
(c) Libraries
(d) India

The above four are uniterm.

Example: Library training in India

It has three concepts:

(a) Library
(b) Training
(c) India

Library is a uniterm heading while training and India are taken out of alphabetical file. These are then compared to identify common document identification numbers of the card carrying next to least postings. Common numbers so obtained are further compared with the numbers of the third card. This process is continued till all the cards are finished with, if components are more than three. The comparison of above cards shows that the document with identification number 3462 is available in all the three uniterm cards.

Search for coordination

Libraries

0	1	2	3	4	5	6	7	8	9
		2			5				
20									
	11	42	213			296	517	388	29
				54	275				
140							1597		
	2121	3462							

Training

0	1	2	3	4	5	6	7	8	9
		52						78	
			63	24		166			
30	111	172						188	
		3462							

India									
0	1	2	3	4	5	6	7	8	9
								68	
20		32	63		15		87		29
50	151	62	43	64					
						296	117	445	99
		3462							

It can be presumed that the common document with number 3462 covers all the concepts of the subject and is co-extensive with the subject of query. With the help of this common identification number, further details about the documents dealing with the subject can be found out from the accession file or from the document profile.

Process of isolation of uniterm

Title of Document	Document Identification	Uniterm
Export of wheat to Pakistan	1118	Export, Wheat, Pakistan
Libraries and Society	2221	Libraries, Society
Management of Libraries in India	1597	Management, Libraries, India
Training for Running Libraries in India	3462	Training, Libraries, India

Merits

1. No classification system is required to organize the documents index by uniterm. Those are arranged by their accession numbers.
2. As documents are arranged according to their accession numbers, retrieving the requisite documents is simple and easy.
3. The work at the indexing state is simple as the coordination of subject components is done at the output stage.
4. Since system is simple and uses natural language, the users can understand it without difficulty and can make use of it easily.

5. The physical size of the index can be kept within manageable limits by accommodating a number of items in a single uniterm card.
6. This system can be computerized.

Limitations

1. The limitation of the card size is a serious problem. Limited number of documents can be entered on a single uniterm card. It is difficult to maintain beyond 10,000 documents.
2. The system involves two-stage search:
   (a) The search for document identification number from the uniterm cards.
   (b) The search for document or document on the subject with the help of the above identification number.
3. Arrangement of documents by accession order means that approach must always be made through the index.
4. There is a false coordination in this system.

Chain Indexing

2

Chain Indexing or chain procedure is a mechanical method employed by Dr. Ranganathan to derive subject index entries or subject headings from the class number of documents. Ranganathan has never accepted the marking and parking role of classification. The system was given a fair trial by the British National Bibliography until 1970.

Bhattacharya defined Chain indexing as a systematic method of deriving subject headings for a specific subject, involving the determination of chain in which the subject concerned is the last sought link. The concept of "chain" in the context of universe of subject is the foundation of chain procedure.

A chain is said to be a modulated sequence of sub class or isolated ideas. Chain is derived from classification scheme.

Guha said "If an analytico-synthetic scheme of classification, having a structured notational system, is used in co-extensive representation of a subject, then a retranslation of the class number, using the schedules of the same scheme of classification would give a nearly structured formulation of the subject".

However, chain indexing is a systematic index in which subject headings are derived out of the chain procedure from the classification numbers (class numbers) of a scheme of classification. These subject headings used for indexing are selected or sought subject headings having specific characteristics, suitable to users. These are multidimensional headings.

The name of subject is called class number in notational plane and subject heading in verbal plane. Two types of subjects are derived (1) subject of information sources and (2) subject of user's query.

Dr. Ranganathan defined the chain procedure as the procedure for deriving subject word entry from a class number, in a more or less mechanical way. This method is used to derive Class Index Entry (i.e. Subject Index Entries) in classified catalogue and specific subject entries, subject analytical and "see also" subject entries in dictionary catalogue.

2.1 Characteristics of Chain Indexing

1. There is explicit use of classificatory base.
2. It uses classificatory language.
3. There is hardly an idea of marking and parking function of classification.
4. Indexing language represents specific subject co-extensively.
5. The central idea is the concept of facets and fundamental categories.

2.2 How Chain Procedure Evolved

In an analytico synthesis scheme of classification, there is co-extensive representation of the subject than a translation of the class number using the schedule of the same scheme of classification. Colon is a scheme of structural notation which gives a structural formation of subject. Every subject has some constituent which is a result analysed reflecting the structure. Analysis is the work of the indexer.

Ranganathan was always in favour of classified arrangement. He first applied the chain procedure to a class number and applied on DDC class number. First, he practiced on compound subject and then the basic subjects like Economics, History. But at later stage he applied chain procedure to complex subjects. He named this method 'chain procedure because it forms a chain while analyzing a class number. He enunciated rules about pattern of subject headings and discussed in his book "Theory of Library Catalogue" in 1938.

Chain Procedure is a chain or the sequence of the constituent of the subject derived by analysis out of the class number by a indexer to formulate subject headings.

2.3 Steps in Chain Indexing

There are nine steps in chain indexing:

1. Determining of the specific subject of the document. It is done following the title of the document.
2. Expressing the name of the subject or specific subject of the document in natural language in terms. Ranganathan called this step "Expressive name of subject".
3. Representation of the name of the specific subject in terms of its components or fundamental constituents. In other words representation of specific subject in Kernel terms.
4. Determining fundamental components or constituents in categories and status and position of their role according to the set of postulates and principles formulated for the purpose. This is an "Analysis of the name of subject".
5. After the subject is analysed, it is transformed by proper arrangement of the components or the constituents. This step is "Transformation of the analysed name of subject".
6. Sixth step is a standardization of each term in transformed name of subject. If the standard term is not adequate in the scheme of classification, it should be replaced with the help of the schedule of classification scheme or the glossary or thesaurus. This step is called "Name of subject in standard term".
7. Determination of upper link of the chain. When the name of the subject is allotted standard term, each link is determined. But the first of the upper link is most important link.

   First link is always from the first digit. These links may be determined as under:

   (a) First digit—First link.

   (b) Other digits—Other links in succession.

   (c) Write links one below the other.

(d) Each link is translated in natural language.

(e) Connect each link with the translation.

8. Determination of different kinds of links. These links are known as:

   (a) Sought link (through which a user approaches his document).

   (b) Missing link.

   (c) False link (which is not a class number).

   (d) Unsought link (which ends with a part of isolate focus in a class number. It represents a subject on which reading material is hardly produced or sought, which is not likely to be looked by the reader).

9. Derivation of subject heading. Subject headings are derived on the basis of sought links in chain.

We can enumerate 9 steps as under:

1. Specific subject (Title).
2. Expressive name of the subject.
3. Kernel terms.
4. Analysed name of subject.
5. Transformed title.
6. Standard terms.
7. Determination of upper link.
8. Determination of different kinds of links.
9. Derivation of subject headings.

2.4 Working of Chain Indexing

There are some factors to be considered while processing the chain indexing.

1. All concept terms need not be mentioned.
2. The terms which reveal the correct context are to be considered.
3. The term corresponding to the last digit in the chain is to be mentioned first to use as entry element. This method is called Reverse rendering.

4. There is a system of reference. The specific subject heading (last link) is available to such readers who have the same subject in mind, and express it.
5. If search formulation is not exactly in the form of specific subject headings, the researcher would get it directly.

Example: Treatment of Disease of Retina in children.

The Chain

1. Disease, Retina, Child, Medicine
2. Retina, Eye, Child, Medicine
3. Eye, Child, Medicine
4. Child Medicine
5. Medicine

Nearest match where reader can look for:

Retina disease in children and their treatment
Retina, Eye, Child Medicine

Important aspect of search:

Disease, Treatment

Reference Entry

RETINA, EYE, CHILD, MEDICINE
See also

TREATMENT, DISEASE, RETINA, CHILD, MEDICINE

Chain indexing is a procedure for deriving alphabetical subject headings through digit by digit interpretation of a class number of a document. A class number generates a series of links forming a chain.

Class Number 0111, 1M56

0	=	Literature	(Sought link)
01	=	Teutonic, Literature	(Unsought link)
011	=	Indo-European, Literature	(Unsought link)
0111	=	English, Literature	(Sought link)
0111, 0	=	False link	
0111, 1	=	Poetry, English, Literature	(Unsought link)
0111,1M56	=	Whitman, Poetry, English	(Sought link)

In the above chain

0	=	Literature is known as upper link
0111, 1M56	=	Mr. Whitman, Poetry, English is the lower link.

Subject Headings

Mr. Whitman, Poetry, English	=	0111, 1M56
Poetry, English, Literature	=	0111, 1
English, Literature	=	0111
Literature	=	0

Nationalisation of Banks of India

Specific subject	:	Nationalisation of Banks in India
Expressive title	:	Nationalisation of Banks in India, Economics
Kernal Terms	:	Nationalisation, Banks, India, Economics
Analysed name of the subject	:	Nationalisation (Spl.). Bank (P) India (S) Economics (BC)
Transformed Title	:	Economics (BC) Bank (P) Public Enterprise (Spl.) India (S)
Standard Terms	:	Economics (BC) Bank (P) Public Enterprises (Spl) India (S)
Determination of Upper links	:	X(BC) 62 (P) 9W(Spl) 44(S)
Classified Entry	:	X9W.62.44

Subject headings:

India Banks, Public enterprise. Economic	X9w, 62, 44
Bank, Public enterprise, Economics	X9w, 62
Public Enterprises. Economics	X9w
Economics	X

2.5 Postulation-Based Chain Procedure

Chain procedure is class based system. It is dependent on class number. In other words it depends on postulates about the structure of Name-of-subject forming the foundation of the design and developing of the scheme.

In 1953, A. Thomson suggested the developments in the method of chain procedure. He gave some directions. His system was based on analysis of name-of-subject into six elementary constituents:

(a) Realisation

(b) Material

(c) Process

(d) Problem

(e) Place

(f) Time and form

Ranganathan also further demonstrated how the choice of the name-of-the subject and its rendering by facet analysis based on the set of postulates and principles. It followed artificial language for subject headings.

E.J. Coates used chain procedure for the alphabetical subject index and for derivation of subject headings for British Technology Index. He examined the problems of unsought headings. In this he dealt with the role of the chain procedure.

G. Bhattacharya incorporated classified Cat. System in dictionary catalogue system by developing POPSI.

2.6 Application in Dictionary Catalogue

Ranganathan and E.J. Coates applied idea of chain procedure to be used as a process of deriving subject heading for dictionary catalogue. He demonstrated the system of chain procedure for preparation of multiple subject headings for alphabetico-specific catalogue. POPSI is supposed to be an effective version of chain procedure.

Computerised Chain Procedure

With the introduction of computer for information retrieval, there has been a new development in chain procedure. There will be no need to provide different entries for different approach for specific subject, but single entry will incorporate all necessary points of approach. Computer may help in:

(a) Query specifications and formalisation.

(b) Search

(c) Delivering the output according to specification of the user.

(d) Deriving the subject reference entries.

(e) For delivering the output with a subject index.

Merits

1. The classifier analyses the subject of a document.
2. Classes are retranslated to provide alphabetical approach through class index entries.
3. Chain procedure is based on classification number and terminology given in schedule.
4. This procedure is more suitable for analytico-synthetic scheme of classification.
5. Chain indexing can be applied to any classification scheme in which notation symbols indicate the subordination of each step of division.
6. It provides alternative approach to the classified file through reverse rendering. It helps in retrieving the information of the user.

Application

1. In 1950 B.N.B. adopted chain procedure based on class number constructed based on DDC. In 1971, this version of chain procedure has been discontinued and modified based on the set of postulates and principles. This system is known as PRECIS.
2. INB is adopting this chain procedure since its inception but with some modifications on class number of DDC (16th ed.).

POPSI (Postulate-Based Permutation Subject Indexing)

3

3.1 POPSI (Postulate-Based Permutation Subject Indexing)

It is postulate based permutation subject indexing based on general theory of classification involving postulates and principles. POPSI is an improved version of chain indexing.

It is an indexing procedure. It is a multipurpose system to:

1. formulate subject headings;
2. derive subject index entries;
3. determine the subject of reader's query.

3.1.1 Steps

The following steps are involved in this indexing:

Step-1: Verbal presentation: The first step is the derivation of the postulate based verbal subject representation. It is based on postulates and principles of the general theory of classification of Ranganathan. It helps to secure consistency, to determine the upper link, to identify inter-relation between component ideas of subject, to ensure the co-extensive expression of the subject.

Step-2: Display of components: It involves the determination of the pattern of display of the components of the verbal representation.

Step-3: Short display: Determination of necessary and sufficient component terms to be retained in the verbal presentation to be used for specific purpose.

Step-4: Approach term: Determination, on the basis of full representation of the component ideas, the names of which are likely to be used as 'Approach term' by readers in their search for information about the subject represented.

Step-5: Deriving subject index entries: Deriving subject index entries from the full subject representation in such a way that each of the approach terms occurs as a lead term of the entries.

Step-6: Display of subject index entries: The choice of method, pattern, format for the display of each subject index entry derived by the procedure selected at step 5.

Step-7: Cross references: Determination of the pattern of subject cross referencing in the alphabetical subject index.

Step-8: Alphabetical arrangement of articles: Arrangement of subject index entries and subject cross reference index entries in an alphabetical sequence in a single file.

In view of the above, the process is completed in several steps:

1. Analysis
2. Formalisation
3. Standardisation
4. Modulation
5. Preparation of entries for organizing classification
6. Decision about terms of approach.
7. Preparation of entries for associative classification
8. Alphabetisation

Six steps—based on postulates

Seventh step—based on technique of permutation

Process

Example: Oral streptomycin treatment of human tuberculosis: An evaluation of undesirable effects.

Step-1: Verbal representation: (Derivation of postulate based verbal subject)—After determining the component ideas in the subject:

(a) Linking up these ideas into sub-structures.
(b) Putting the components in the helpful sequence within each sub-structure.

(c) Arranging the sub-structure in helpful sequence among themselves.

Medicine, Human body > Respiratory system > Lung: [Disease-Bacteria > Mycobacterium > Mycrobecterium tuberculosis] = Tuberculosis: Treatment—Drug > Antibiotic > Streptomycin—Route of administration > Oral; Effects side-effects > Undesirable effects: Evaluation.

Note: > Symbol denotes inclusion relation

- Subordinate links of each specific are as represented
- All components are arranged in helpful sequence
- Words and symbols are used to show the sequence and relationship among the components in the subject representation

Step-2: Display of components: We are considering display of bibliographical tools, such as catalogue or documentation list. Hence, display has to be linear.

Step-3: The full representation prepared in Step-1 can now be reduced to following name-of-subject

Medicine, Lung: Tuberculosis: Treatment—streptomycin—oral administration; undesirable effects: Evaluation.

Step-4: Selection of approach term is to be made from the representation of the subject as mentioned in Step-1. In addition, the alternative terms and synonyms of the component terms are also to be taken care of.

i.e. 'Therapeutics' and 'therapy' may be considered alternative terms for 'treatment'. Similarly, 'side reaction' is term used synonymously for 'side effect.

Step-5: Subject index entries are to be derived from the full subject representation such that each of the approach term selected occurs as lead term of the entries.

Step-6: A preferred method of display of the subject index entry may consist of three selections:

Section 1 Lead term section

Section 2 Subject representation section

Section 3 Reference section

- The lead term section gives Lead Term and its immediate context in which the idea denoted by Lead Term occurs in the subject concerned.
- Short display of subject as stated in Step-3 is given.
- The Reference section gives class number or any other identification number of the document.

EVALUATION, UNDESIRABLE EFFECTS

Medicine, Lung; Tuberculosis: Treatment—Streptomycin-oral; undesirable effects: Evaluation

LUNG, MEDICINE

Medicine, Lung; Tuberculosis: Treatment—streptomycin-oral; undesirable effects: Evaluation

DRUG, TREATMENT, TUBERCULOSIS

Medicine, Lung; Tuberculosis: Treatment—streptomycin-oral; undesirable effect: Evaluation

Step-7: Cross Reference

'See' Reference entries are prepared for each of the alternative, near-synonymous and synonymous terms for the component terms in the subject representation; and cross reference entries (see also) references are to be prepared for each of the closely related or collateral idea or subject.

Therapeutics *see* Treatment

Therapy *see* Treatment

Streptopennicillin *see also* Streptomycin

Step-8: Alphabetical arrangement

The following entries are prepared and arranged in alphabetical sequence:

(a) Subject Index Entries

(b) Subject Cross Reference Entries

(c) Subject Cross Reference Index Entries

3.1.2 Bhattacharya's interpretation

Step-1 Analysis of the Subject Indicative Expression (Analysis).

Step-2 Formalisation of subject-proposition (formalisation).

Step-3 Standardisation of subject-proposition.

Step-4 Modulation of the subject-proposition.

Step-5 Preparation of entry for organizing classification.

Step-6 Decision about terms of approach.

Step-7 Preparation of entries for associative classification.

Step-8 Alphabetical arrangement of entries.

3.1.3 Recent modifications

Bhattacharya made some modifications. A new set of Elementary categories has been recommended. They are:

D (Discipline)

E (Entity)

A (Action)

P (Property)

M (Modified)

D (Discipline)—It includes conventional field of study, or any aggregate of such field, *e.g.* Physical Science, Physics, Chemistry, etc.

E (Entity)—This elementary catalogue includes manifestations having perceptual correlates, or only concept existence, as contrasted with their properties, and action performed by them or on them, *e.g.* energy, light, plant, animals, place, time, environment, etc.

A (Action)—An elementary catagory that includes manifestations denoting the concept of 'doing'.

P (Property)—An elementary category that includes manifestations denoting the concept of "attributes"—qualitative or quantitative, *e.g.* property, effect, power, capability, efficiency, utility, form, etc.

M (Modified)—In relation to a manifestation any one of the elementary category D, E, A and P, the term modifier refers to an idea used or intended to be used to qualify manifestation without disturbing the conceptual wholeness of the latter, *e.g.* "Infectious" in "Infectious disease".

Subject—"Chemical treatment of the adenocarcinoma of stomach":

D = Medicine (Implicit)

E = Stomach (Explicit)

E = Adenocarcinoma (Explicit)

A on P = Chemical treatment (Explicit) = (chemotherapy)

Medicine 6 man, Digestive System, Stomach

6.2 Disease cancer carcinoma, Adenocarcinoma

6.2.1 Treatment, Chemotherapy

6 stands for entity, 6.2.1 for Action (A and P), A comma (,) between terms indicates part whole relationship and a stop (.) indicates species/type relationship.

A typical index entity derived from the above will be—Digestive System.

Medicine 6, Man, Digestive System, Stomach 6.2

Disease, Cancer, Carcinoma, Adevocarcinoma

6.2.1 Treatment Chemotherapy.

3.1.4 Quality

1. The basic version of POPSI is readily amenable to transformation into any specific version to meet specific requirements through a set of standardized rules and decision about the Base and Core.
2. The basic version of POPSI
   (a) Make provision for all possible term of approach.
   (b) Ensures organizing classification in general, more or less, under each term-of-approach.
3. The basic version of POPSI helps its users to ascertain at any point-of-approach.
4. It may be computerised.

PRECIS (Preserve Context Indexing System)

4

The most important alphabetical approach to subject specification that has been developed is PRECIS. It was designed and developed by British National Bibliography in 1971. There are a few characteristics of this system. Derck Austin developed PRECIS. BNB used chain procedure for a few years in the beginning for the purpose of class subject entries, but after the emergence of MARC project and the involvement of BNB, it was felt to derive some other method which can be used with MARC format in the exchange of data on magnetic tapes on reciprocal basis with the Library of Congress. Chain procedure could work with Dewey Decimal Classification in generating the subject index entries. MARC record was having class number for each item in DC and LC but none of these could be proved proper and accurate and could not represent fully the contents of a document since these records were meant to be exchanged internationally, it was necessary that a full subject specification should be available for each document included.

Keeping in view the problems of chain procedure, PRECIS was developed by BNB for preparing MARC record.

Definition

According to Derek Austin—

Precis is a system in which the initial string terms, organized according to a scheme of role operators, is computer manipulated so that related words function in term as the approach term. Entries are restructured at every step in such a way that the user can determine from the layout of the entry which terms set the appropriate term into its context and which terms are context dependent on the approach term.

PRECIS present alphabetical subject index for each and every term which together make up a compound statement and establish at that point the full text in which his chosen term has been considered by the author.

According to KGB Blackwell—

PRECIS is a system of subject indexing which provides a full subject statement at each significant point of entry in the index. The context of the terms is always preserved and each index entry is co-extensive with the subject indeed. All entries except one have a two-line structure reflecting the following pattern—

LEAD		QUALIFIER
	DISPLAY	

4.1 Objectives

PRECIS has following objectives—

1. The index entries generated by the system are meaningful, which help the user to interpret them correctly.
2. The system avoids unnatural entries and inverted headings.
3. Computer cannot destore the meaning and the generated entries during manipulation of the input string.
4. The system is to be independent of any scheme of classification.
5. Subject headings are to be co-extensive with the contents of the document at all access points.
6. References are adequately arranged between semantically related terms.
7. The system is flexible as it accommodates the new terms freely which are put into the literature.

4.2 Precis Process

Term—Term is a verbal representation of a concept consisting of one or more words.

An ordered sequence of component is called a string. The string represents the subject of the document.

Role Operation—The Role operators are the code symbols which show the functions of the component terms and fix its position in the strings.

4.2.1 Strings

Two principles are followed in preparation of string:

(a) One to one relation

(b) Context dependence

When component terms are arranged in the string, they are context dependent to each other. String term's meaning depends on the meaning of the term used preceding the term and expresses the single context together. This is called one-to-one relationship with each component term of the string.

Term + String + Term = 1 + 3 with single context
(1) (2) (3)

(1) + 3 = one to one relation.

Example: 1

Selection of staff in the libraries of India.
Selection, staff, libraries, India.
Relationship—India. Libraries. Staff. Selection.
Selection → staff → Libraries
(Term) (String) (Terms + context)
(Selection of staff in libraries of India)

Example: 2

Training of skilled Personnel in Indian Textile Industries.
Training. Textile Industries. Skilled persons.
(Term) (Strong) (Term+context)
India

Training of skilled persons in textile industries of India.

4.2.2 Role operators

Role operators help in the writing of the strings in PRECIS. Input terms are prefixed by a role operator. It plays a role in this context. Role operators also serve as computer instructions for determining—

(a) Format
(b) Typography
(c) Punctuation

Role Operators of Precis

Mainline operators	0 Location
Environment of observed Systems	1 Key system: object of transitive action; agent of intransitive action.
Observed system core Operators	2 Action/Effect
	3 Agent of transitive action: Aspects: Factors
A	
Data relating to observer	4 Viewpoint-as-form
Selected instance	5 Sample population/study region
Presentation of data	6 Target/Form
Interposed operators Depended elements	p part/property q member of guasi-generic group r Aggregate
Concept interlinks	s Role definer t Author attributed association
Coordinate concept	g coordinate concept
B	
Differencing operators (prefixed by $)	h Non-lead direct difference i Lead direct difference j Silent difference k Non-lead indirect difference m Lead indirect difference n Non-lead parenthetical difference

Contd...

	o Lead parenthetic difference
	d Data as a difference
Connectives (components of linking phrases; prefixed by $)	v Downward reading component
	w Upward reading component
C	
Theme interlinks	x First element in Coordinate theme
	y Subsequent element in coordinate theme
	z Element of common theme

Step-1: Indexer determines the thought contents of the documents. The thought content of the document will consist of a title-like phrase.

Example: Training of skilled personnel in the Indian textile Industries.

Step-2:

1. The syntactic (वाक्य रचना) role of the component concept are determined.
2. Relevant operators which express these roles are assigned to the concept terms.

Step-3: Process of determining the syntactical roles—

1. The indexer needs to examine this phrase to know the action of term.
2. The action will determine how the rest of the subjects are handled similar to the role of term in a sentence. (Sentence cannot be completed without a verb).

   Hence—

   Training denotes the action and, therefore, term should be prefixed by the operator (2).

Step-4: Indexer has to determine the kind of action—

1. By represented by the term "Training".

2. By distinguishing between 'transitive' and 'intransitive' action.

   Training is clearly a transitive action. It fulfils the object.

3. The indexer searches the concept which is semantically related as the object of transitive action.
4. The object is frequently coded in key system (operator 1). Skilled personnel is a string and appear in the form:

   (i) Skilled personnel

   (ii) Training

5. Skilled personnel are the part of some other named system, i.e. "Textile Industries".
6. There is a whole part relationship (skilled personnel + Textile industries) called, the interposed operator and can be used as:

   (1) Textile Industries

   (P) Skilled Personnel

   (2) Training

7. The term which leads 'India' should be coded, which functions as the environment. This is introduced by operator 'O'.

   (o) India

   (1) Textile Industries

   (p) Skilled personnel

   (2) Training

Step-5: Computer—

1. The computer will recognize this 0-1-2 pattern of operators as a standard sequence called shunting operation compared to rotation of keywords.
2. It is related to non-numerical operator.
3. The phrase (p) skilled personnel has been attached to (1) Textile industry to which it is more related.
4. Thus every string must contain at least one concept which is introduced by—(a) the operator (1) representing

a thing or (b) else the operator (2) which projects the action.

5. String is the most significant aspect of PRECIS.
6. Computer will generate the following set of entries -
   India
   Textile industries. Skilled personnel. Training
   Textile Industries. India
   Skilled personnel. Training

   Skilled personnel. Textile industrics. India. Training
   Training. Skilled personnel. Textile industries. India

Step-6: Enhancing the complexity of this subject

Complexity of the subject may be enhanced generating extra dependent elements at various points in the string.

Example: If the subject is related to Mumbai:

(o) India (Note upward)

(p) Mumbai

(1) Textile industry

(p) Skilled personnel

(2) Training

Example: If the study is related to women:

(o) India (NU)

(p) Mumbai

(1) Textile Industries

(p) Skilled personnel

(q) Women

(2) Training

Step-7: Subject of exposition of document

1. Containers $i
   Polystyrene $ expanded
   (i) Container is focus.
   (ii) Polystyrene directly refers to container.
   — Hence, it is called 'direct difference' and is indicated by the differencing operator 'i'.

— the term 'expanded' refers to polystyrene and not to the focus, that is containers. Hence it is called 'Indirect difference' and is indicated by 'm'.

Example:

Containers
    Expanded polystyrene containers
Polystyrene containers
    Expanded polystyrene containers
    Expanded polystyrene containers

2. Use of sole definer and connectives in the string

(i) role definer—operator 's'

(ii) connectives—$v and $w

Example:

India
    Textile industries. Skilled personnel. Training
    Role of consultants

(Last entry)

    Consultants. Textile industries. India
    Role in training of skilled personnel

Example:

1. Political aspects of university manpower planning.

Entries -

EDUCATION
    University. Manpower. Planning. Political aspects
UNIVERSITY. Education
    Manpower. Planning. Political aspects
MANPOWER. University education
    Planning. Political aspects
PLANNING. Manpower. University education.
    Political aspects.

2. Document: In service training of women skilled personnel in cement industries in Bombay string:

(o) India

(p) Mumbai

(1) Cement Industry
(p) Skilled personnel
(q) Women
(2) Training

INDIA

Mumbai. Cement industries. Skilled personnel: Women. In-service training

MUMBAI

Cement industries skilled personnel. Women. In-service training.

CEMENT INDUSTRIES. MUMBAI

Skilled personnel: Women. In-service training

WOMEN. Skilled personnel cement industries. Bombay

Women. In-service training

TRAINING. Women. Skilled personnel

Cement industry. In-service training.

IN-SERVICE TRAINING. Women. Skilled personnel.

Cement industries. Mumbai

Chain Procedure	POPSI	PRECIS
1. Chain word is vague. 2. No symbols for relation in chain. 3. No efforts to avoid ambiguities. 4. Chain eliminates one term in its entries. 5. It failed to give more information. 6. Classified file is consulted as a	1. It has got the limitation. 2. It is not based on any scheme of classification as chain indexing. 3. It uses the idea and theory of classification. 4. It follows the analysis of subjects and structuring of the name of the subjects.	1. It permits the use to enter the alphabetical subject index. 2. Alphabetical subject is at any one point of the significant terms. 3. Terms together make up a (cds) and establish at that point. At that point full context of the chosen term by the author.

Chain Procedure	POPSI	PRECIS
basis of selection. 7. It does not give full compound sentence. 8. It need not have any adequate terminology. 9. It has an economy of order. 10. Role operators of PRECIS seem to be the same as Ranganathan's Fundamental Categories. 11. Syntactic structure of PRECIS is similar to freely faced structure based on context dependency.	5. POPSI has increased the possibilities of deeper analysis and also analysis for different purposes. 6. It has used indicator digits, in the full presentation of subjects as an additional syntactical device. 7. It has also used better format and methods of display of entries than the chain indexing.	4. PRECIS includes all terms (elements in a cds) in each index entry. 5. Full compound sentence is indexed at each step. 6. It gives more information than chain. 7. It refers to rotation in terms. 8. It depends on adequacy of terminology. 9. It has no economy of order. 10. PRECIS shows influence of Ranganathan like postulation approach, facet analysis, etc.

4.3 Keyword Indexing

Special Types of Indexes

KWIC (Keyword in Context)

This indexing system is based on the principle that the title of the scientific document represents its contents. The title as presumed is one-line abstract of the document. In KWIC indexing, an entry is made under each significant word in the title. It is done because:

(a) It brings it in turn along with the remaining part of the title to keep the context intact;

(b) Keywords are in natural language. They serve as approach terms by turn; and

(c) Keywords also maintain the context for each display.

Mr. H.P. Luhu of IBM developed the completely mechanized indexing system which was named KWIC index. KWIC index is essentially produced by the rotation of all the significant terms in the titles. There is hardly any intellectual effort involved in it. But it involves:

(a) proper manipulation of title

(b) generation of multiple entries

(c) arrangement by the computer

(d) formatting by the computer

(e) certain techniques and programming skills.

KWIC index consists of three steps:

1. Keyword selection
2. Entry generation
3. Filing

4.3.1 Keyword selection

Significant words or keywords are selected in the first instance—articles, prepositions, conjunctions and other non-significant words are omitted.

Example:

Cataloguing of periodicals in university libraries of India.

Significant words—Cataloguing, Periodicals, University, Libraries, India.

Non-significant words—of, in, of

First keywords are marked by the indexer or editor. Computer is used for preparing the index.

4.3.2 Generation of entries

Each significant word in title serves as keyword in turn. The title avoiding non-significant keywords provides the complete context to the keywords serving access points to the search.

The location of a document is indicated by identification code on the extreme right.

When the computer moves and entries are generated, the computer moves the title literally in such a way that a significant word for a particular entry always appears either on the extreme left hand side or in the centre of the columns. Non-significant words are automatically omitted and no entry is generated to them.

4.3.3 Filing

After all the index entries are generated, each entry is filed at its appropriate place in the alphabetical sequence.

KWIC index consists of 3 parts:

1. Keyword
2. Context
3. Identification number or code number of each keyword in turn.

Remaining part of the title is context of keywords. A sign either/ or = indicates the end of the title.

Example: Document No. 1123

Title: Classification of books in a university library.

Entries—

BOOKS in a University library / classification of	1123
CLASSIFICATION of books in a university library	1123
LIBRARY/Classification of books in a university	1123
UNIVERSITY library / classification of books in a	1123

Example:

Document Acquisition of books in libraries

ACQUISITION of books in a library	1540
BOOKS in a library / Acquisition of	1540
LIBRARY / Acquisition of books	1540
or	
in a library / ACQUISITION of books	1540
Acquisition of BOOKS in a library	1540
of books in a LIBRARY/Acquisition	1540

Citation Index

5

5.1 What is Citation

The lowly footnotes have now attained a position of considerable importance. The determination of footnotes or citation practice is not easy. According to Derek de Solla Price, the earlier name of a footnote was 'schelia' which means "relating to scholarship". Footnote writing was a scholarly work. Barr gave an example that in a scholarly poem of 14 pages, 20 references were given. Most of the references were shown as 'Ibid' that was dubbed as a 'Garland of 'ibids'.'

The primary purpose of a citation is to enable a reader to go to the referred to document for more information on a point or check the authority of a particular view, finding and method. Citation is considered as message of the author of a document to its readers.

5.1.1 Citation as bibliography

Citation list may be used as reading list. It is available in newly developed topic in the form of bibliography. Ranganathan compared citation as 'Plums of Sevari" which are offered to Lord Rama. In the same way the citations used by authors mean distribution to his readers. Citations are also useful to bibliographer, librarians and documentalists. The authors' style is generally reflected in their writings through citations as these citations reflect the reading pattern of community.

Similarly the rank list of periodicals and a subject can be used in the selection of periodicals for acquisition in a library. Such list is also helpful for planning the coverage of an abstracting and indexing service. Generally, research workers depend more and more on articles in periodicals, reports, conference proceedings, etc. than on books. The quantitative measure of their relative importance is necessary. A rough measure can be provided by citation studies. About 80% citations are the periodicals. This provides the importance of the document. It guides the libraries to allocate their budget based on importance of documents, i.e. books and journals or the other document. We can also measure the rate of progress of a respective subject. Browen's study had shown their citation of serials in Physics where two volumes of periodicals were published in last 10 years was 75.6%, while it was 33.9% in Zoology. Hence, citation helps in determining the policy of acquisition.

Citation index also helps in determining the relationship importance among the subjects in applied science. No subject has a permanent value by:

(a) The ranked list of periodicals.
(b) Age distribution of citations.
(c) Evidence of relative importance of different types of subjects.

The validity of relative importance is for a certain period only. Fresh citation studies are made from time to time to measure the importance of the document. Such comparative studies help to bring into focus the rise and fall in the use frequency and the popularity of the documents, periodicals, etc.

Citation indexing is based on the assumptions:

(a) A document giving citations of the previously published document indicates subject relationship between the current documents and the old documents.
(b) The documents which cite the same publication have some subject relationship with each other.

The institute for scientific information, Philadelphia, USA (An ISI institute) has given the working of citation indexing:

Researchers support the current articles in comparison to previously published articles to classify or refer to the method and procedure, support or criticise the previous researcher, to indicate alternative directions, and appraise the good research articles.

5.1.2 Traditional method of citation

An inverted file of all documents is constructed on the basis of subject terms. This inverted file was based on the citations from a document. In other words inverted file is a list of all documents cited in a particular year. This list became the source of further citations. The main object of citation indexing is to focus the subject through the author and title by linking the two and taking them as chains in subject linkage.

Development

The idea of citation index came in the mind of Frank Shephard of USA. The first citation index was "Frank Shephard's Citation Index" in 1973. It proved fruitful to lawyers to base their arguments on previous judgements on similar point of law. In 1952, Welch Project concerned itself with the indexing of medical literature. He applied Shephard's technique for indexing of scientific literature. Engens Garfield was the second scholar who wrote a few articles on the importance of citation indexing and employed this method for bibliographical control of scientific literature. The first 'Science Citation Index' (SCI) was brought out in 1961 and 'Genetic Citation Index' in 1963.

There were other citation indexes, i.e.:

(a) Cumulative index to the journal of the American Statistical Association Vols. 35-50 in 1959.

(b) The Bibliography of Non-parametric statistics, 1962.

(c) Citation Index was given in journal of Herto Chemist and Cytochemistry, 1968.

(d) Law Review Citation (Shephard).

(e) Citation Index for statistics and probability by Dr. J.W. Tukey, 1971.

(f) Shephard's Citation Index.

(g) Shephard's Science Citation Index.

(g) Shephard's Social Science Citation Index.

5.1.3 Citation index

Citation Index is an index whose term consists of citations from the documents being indexed. Essentially, it is a method of detecting the relationship of documents through citation. If a recent paper cites the earlier paper, it is assumed that there is some association of ideas between the citing and cited paper. This association is converted in the form of an index keeping the direction from the cited to the citing documents. In other words, the author of the paper citing someone else's work in reference has found some relationship between the subject matter of the cited work and that of his own. In scientific papers, an author refers the earlier works which are related to his subject while writing a paper. The citations which the author makes to other papers are utilized as index headings. Scientific articles usually quote a number of sources of references. A citation index is thus a list of cited documents arranged under each cited document. A cited document is one to which the reference is made and the citing document is that which makes reference to the cited document.

Citation index is tremendously successful in law as much as it is based on precedents. As an inventory, the citation index collects at one place bibliographical descendants of a given cited case and the searcher in the legal literature is automatically led from a given case of reference to several later cases.

Ranganathan, S.R. Classified Catalogue Code. Index. Madras Lib. Asso., 1945.

5.2 Citing Document

Bhattacharya, G. "Relative Index and Chain Procedure". Lib. Sc. Doct. 8, 369 (1971)

Neelmeghan, A. "Chain procedure and micro subject".

Codes, E.J. "Chain procedure; application in British Technology Index", Electrotechnology, 8(1), 33 (1964).

Doughty, D.W. "Chain procedure subject indexing and featuring a classified catalogue". LAS, 57, 141 (1955).

The above articles cited the book of Ranganathan in their papers published in various journals in various years. The full bibliographical citations giving reference to the paper in which the citation appeared, recorded in machine-processible form, permits ready manipulation by computer to produce listing ready for user's consultations.

Books are macro thoughts and articles are micro-thoughts. If citation index deals with both, it may be called sub-micro or molecular unit of thought. Such index, i.e. 'Thought" index are very useful if they are properly conceived and developed.

Citation index helps

(a) to overcome the problem of changing terminology;
(b) in achieving a pastoriori indexing because citation is an experimental method;
(c) in identifying the significance of the literature;
(d) to highlight evaluate the literature, theories which become outdated and need to be revised or modified;
(e) in striving more than a straight subject index.

5.2.1 Usefulness

1. Its value to searcher is more enduring than its value to the indexer as it provides a complete case history for each paper.
2. It is reliable on the research practices of a scientist, who knows his subject field, and knows the author of his field and is able to analyse those references which are relevant and highly important to his overall study.
3. Citation Index is a powerful tool for bibliographic control of micro-documents.
4. Index does not follow any logical method, but is built entirely on arbitrary construction.
5. Citation indexing has the potentiality of performing important "evaluation, analytical, and predictive roles" in the scientific, technological and academic settings.
6. Citation Indexing has an independent place in an information retrieval system particularly in generating ideas for innovation.

7. It is an art of finding what one is looking for, it leads the researcher who knows of one relevant paper in the field.
8. Citation written under other disciplines reveals useful combination and unexpected correlation.
9. Citation indexing helps the searcher to cut across disciplines to pull together relational information.
10. Citation index is capable of being computerised by feeding a computer with the citations of each article and then applying an inverse sorting procedures, as the coding consists essentially of clerical operation.

5.2.2 Citation

When a document D1 refers to another document D2 as a source of information,

Or a support for a particular viewpoint,

Or as an authority for a statement of fact,

Or an acknowledgement of an earlier work on which the present work is based,

Or an indication of a related work,

D2 called cited document and a brief description thereof to facilitate its identification and location is called citation.

Citation generally occurs at the end of an article, usually under such heading as 'references'. Sometimes they occur in the form of footnotes.

Example:

Citing Journal	Indian Jrl. of Biochemistry and Biophysics Vol. 28, April 1991; pp. 93-95 Bacteriophase M13 based Sandwich Hybridisation Assey for Detection of Hepatitis B Virus in Human Blood.
Citing Author	Kakali Banerjee & Pramod Khandekar Give Expression Laboratory, National Institute of Immunology. Shahid Jeet Singh Marg, New Delhi-110067.

Cited Author	Cited Journal
1. Southern, E.M. (1975)	J Mol Biol. 98, 503
2. Cunningham M. (1983)	Anal Biochem. 128, 415-421
3. Bowels N.E., Richardson (1986)	P.J. London, 1120-1123
4. Kafetos. F.C., John C.W. (1979)	Nucleic Res. 7, 1541-1552
5. Hu N. & Messing J. (1982)	Gene 17, 271-277
6. Banerjee K., Sharma G. (1989)	J Biosci, 14, 279-287
7. Walter E., Blum H.E. (1987)	Hepatology, 7, 557
8. Laboratory manual for cloning Bethesda Res. Laboratory, USA on sequencing in M13 Bacteriophage	
9. Rigsip P.W.J., Dickmann M (1977)	J Mol Biol 113, 237.

In the above example most of the articles are journal articles and their bibliographical detail comprises name(s) of the author(s), year of publication, Journal's title (in abbreviated form) and inclusive pages. But titles of the articles are not given. In case of books, title of the book/document is normally given. It shows that the pattern of references may vary from journal to journal and from publication to publication. For example, the title of article is given in the references that figure in the Indian Journal of Medical Research.

Citation indexing is based on citation analysis. This is also called as cito-analytical studies. In the above example there is a list of citations in their unit, appended to a research paper figuring in April 1991 issue of Indian Journal of Biochemistry and Biophysics. Now we arrange them chronologically. More than 50% of the citations are less than 10 years old. When we arrange the same cluster of citations according to journals, it shows that about 80% of the citations belong to only about 20% of the journals which shows the preference of a few important journals by the scientists.

If we prepare a ranked list, journals are arranged according to the number of citations received by the journal over a particular period, maybe one year or more.

Rank	One year or more Name of the Journal	No. of citations received by the journal in 1987
1.	J Bial Chem	163605
2.	Nature	155736
3.	Proc Nath Acad Sc. USA	152150
4.	J An Chem Soc	114212
5.	Science	97700
6.	J Chem Phys.	79638
7.	Bio Chem Bio Phy Acts	66819
8.	New England J Med	6628?

5.2.3 Impact factor

The impact factor of the journal implies the frequency with which the average article of the journal has been cited in a particular year.

Normally the citations received by a journal in a particular calendar year for its source item published in a preceding calendar year/s are taken into account for determining the impact factor. Mathematically, we can represent JCR impact factor as:

If (Jy) = Impact factor of the journal J for the year.

x_1 = Number of citations received by y1 source items in the year y.

x_2 = Number of citations received by y2, source item in the year y.

y_1 = Number of source items published in jounal J in the year (y-2).

y_2 = Number of source items published in journal J in (y-1) year.

x_1 and x_2 are value of database which may change with the change in the database.

Example:

Journal of American Society of Information Science (JASIS)

JASIS published 46 and 56 source items in 1987 and 1988, respectively. These source items received 60 and 52 citations in 1989 through the source journals covered in two database of SCI (Science Citation Index).

SSCI (Social Science Citation Index)

$$= \text{If (JASIS 89)} = \frac{60+52}{46+56} = \frac{112}{102} = 1.098$$

Journal of citation report the ranked list of periodicals on Behavioural Science.

Rank	Name of the Journal	Impact factor of 1990
1.	J Bial Rhythm	2367
2.	J Exp Psycho Anim B	2338
3.	Ethol Sociobial	2261
4.	J Ecp. Anal Behoo	1520
5.	Sleep	1508
6.	Physical Behav	1244
7.	Behaviour	1104
8.	Cortex	0867
9.	Hum Factors	0583
10.	Behav Process	0494
11.	Bio Behav	0282

5.2.4 Immediacy index ranked list

Immediacy index is a measure to show how quickly the "average article" of a particular journal is cited, and is expressed by the ratio of the number of citations received in a particular year, by the source items of the journal of the same year, divided by the number of aforesaid source items. Mathematically, it can be expressed as:

$$= I_1 \text{ (Jy)} = \frac{c}{x}$$

Where I_1 (Jy) = Immediacy index of the journal J for the year Y.

C = Number of citations received by x source items published in Journal J in the year Y.

x = Number of source items published in journal J in the year Y.

In Science = 813 source items published in 1987.

- The source items received 2838 citations (SCI, SSCI database) in the year 1987 itself.

$$I_1 \text{ (Science 87)} = \frac{2838}{813} = 3.491$$

Ranked List

Rank	Title	Immediacy Index
1.	Lancet	4832
2.	Scientist	4020
3.	Nature	3903
4.	Cell	3824
5.	Phys Rev Litt	3679
6.	Science	3491
7.	Amu Rev Biochem	3207

Chronological distribution of percentage of citations received by journals

Cited Journal	Lab Anim	Lan Cet	Laser Surg Med.	Lect
1987	1.50	3.38	4.72	5.02
1985	21.11	23.53	50.44	32.44
1983	43.53	42.73	89.18	49.89
1981	61.20	56.03	96.61	64.83
1979	73.27	65.31	100.00	85.12

Cited journals—J Mol Biol. Anal Biochem and Lancet, etc.

5.3 Cumulative Percentage of Citations

Citing journal—Indian Jrl. of Biochemistry and Biophysics

Cited Journal	Lab Anim	Lan Cet	Laser Surg Med.	Lect Note Comp. Sci
1987	0.25	13.12	0.64	2.62
1985	9.16	43.47	24.13	30.86
1983	21.67	60.16	50.11	50.44
1981	34.44	70.10	64.22	63.56
1979	47.09	77.31	72.08	73.11

Rank list of authors (Scientist)—(Most cited of 1967)

Rank	Scientist	Total terms cited
1.	Lowry D H	2921
2.	Chance B	1374
3.	London L D (62 Phys)	1174
4.	Panling L (54 Chem)	1063
5.	Cotton F A	940
6.	Ballancy L J	906
7.	Baker B R	876
8.	Kalthoff I M	853
9.	Hersber G (71 chem)	842
10.	Weber G	750
11.	Mott N F (77 Phys)	741
12.	Freud S	727
13.	Jacob F (65 Med)	711
14.	Winstein S	702
15.	Fieser L F	666
16.	Bates D R	627
17.	Gilman H	618
18.	Glick D	609

5.3.1 Citation profile of a scientist

A scientist conducts research and publishes the results in the form of papers, thesis, etc. Generally, an original work opens up new vistas of study and thereby causes the citation of the original work in later works. Citation given in scientist's work shows the importance of the work in the following terms:

1. Total number of citations of the works in a fixed period of time.
2. The number of citations per paper
3. Percentage of self-citations
4. Percentage of cited papers
5. Yearwise distribution of citations

5.3.2 Citation analysis of research papers (1962-90) of a scientist

Total Papers Analysed	= 61
Number of papers with Citation	= 48 (78.7%)
Total Citations Received	= 687
Maximum Citations Received	= 97 by a paper
Number of papers with 10	= 21 citations
Citations / papers	= 14.31
Self-citations	= 29 (42%)

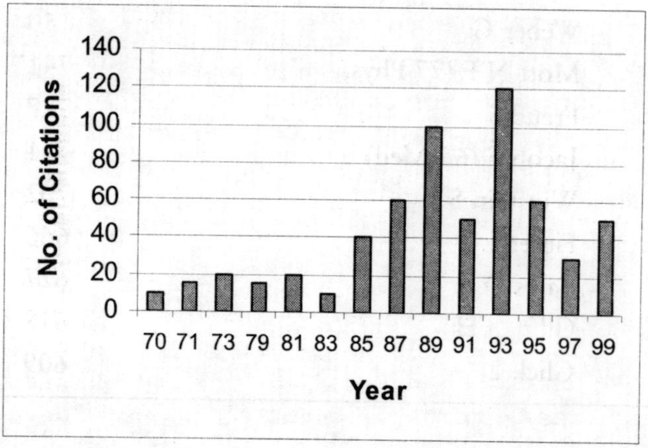

Citation Index

Science Citation Index (Bi-monthly cumulative annually. 1945-54-1955-64, 1965-74.

BOSE A K — Volume Number

Page Number

Cited Author
Year of Publication — 72 TETRAHEDR Litt 40 4091

Eurnal Abbreviation (Cited Index) — CHOTTY CJ JMOL STRUC 218 153 90

PALOMO CJ ORG CHEM 55 2498 90

Citing Author — PALOMO CJ TETRAHEDR L 31 6429 90

Citing Jrl.

RAO SN JAM CHEM 9 1 1 2 2 7 2 9 90

Citing Jrl. Vol. No. Page No. Year of Pub.

73 INDIAN J CHEM 11 896

Agrawal MC Cited both the Papers — 73 J INDIAN CHEM SOC 50 197
AGRAWAL MC JSCI INDR R 49 13 90R

Document is a Review article

73 TETRAHEDRON LETT 3937
KTH TH JORG CHEM 55 3609 90
KOZIKOWS APJ ORG CHEM 30 863 90

5.4 Science Citation Index

Science citation index that was first prepared by Institute for Scientific Information, is a good example of the integrated search system for a comprehensive coverage of the periodical literature in science and technology in general. Engens Garfield introduced this index in 1961 and started regularly bringing out by the Institute of Scientific Information. It also brings out Social Science Citation Index since 1972.

It covers about 3,000 scientific journals and nearby 1,200 books of more than 100 disciplines. It covers the following areas:

(1) Agriculture (2) Biology (3) Environment Sciences (4) Engineering (5) Technology and Applied Science (6) Medical (7) Life Sciences (8) Physical Science (9) Chemical Science (10) Behavioural Science.

In 1963, it used inter-disciplinary database covering literature of calendar year of 1961. It comprised of 5 volumes, covering 613 periodicals and contained 14,00,000 citations. It covered 2,000 periodicals in 1969 and 3,000 in 1972.

Presently this index has three main parts:

(a) Citation Index
(b) Source Index
(c) Permuterm Subject Index

It is published quarterly. It covers 6,00,000 items each year. SCI includes the following documents:

(a) Articles
(b) Short communications
(c) Letters
(d) Reviews
(e) Corrections and errata
(f) Discussions
(g) Conference items
(h) Editorials
(i) Tributes
(j) Obituaries

1. Each year the last issue of December is a cumulative issue for the whole year.
2. Cited documents are arranged alphabetically by the name of the respective first author. Each one of these cited references—presented by the name of the first

author, year, title of the document or the journal, volume, and starting page number—is immediately followed by at least one.

5.4.1 Citation index part

Citing references presented by the name of the first author, title of the source journal, year, volume and starting page number.

1. Cited references
   (a) Name of the first author
   (b) Year
   (c) Title of document/journal
   (d) Volume
   (e) Starting page number
2. Followed by Citina references—
   (a) Name of the first author
   (b) Title of the source journal
   (c) Year
   (d) Volume
   (e) Starting page number
3. If an article in a source journal has cited 10 references then the same article will be featured under each of these is different cited references in citation index.
4. Anonymous cited documents where no personal authorship is attributed are arranged separately alphabetically by the titles of the publication.

Example: 1 (Prasan) Cited author (जिसे उद्धृत किया गया है)

↗

NICHOLS WH

	Publication	Vol.	Page	Citing Year
68 (cited year)				
	J CHEM PHYS	49	1000	
BOON JP	PHYS REVA	2	2542	70
CANDAU S	ANN PHYSIQ	4	21	69
CARDAMON MJ	J OPT SOC L	60	1264	70

5.4.2 Citing journal

1. W.H. Nichols' article published in Journal of Chemical Physics in its Volume No. 49 at page 1000-1007 in 1968.

2. The other article of J.P. Boon which was published in Physics Review A in volume 2 page 2542 in 1970 gave reference or citing the article of WH Nichols which published in 1968.

A ने B का लेख अपनी पत्रिका में संदर्भित किया।

A—Citing document / author

B—Cited document / article

If other words BOON, CANAU and CARDOMON gave reference of W.H. Nichols in their article. It means they are citing the author W.H. Nichols in different journals.

Example: 2 (Guha)

Cited Author	Cited Year	Publication	Citing Year	Vol.	Page
URAY H.C.	31	PHYS REV		38	1969
PILLAI M.G.K.		AUST J. CHEM	65	42	1952
TADOKORO H.		J. CHEM PHYS	65	42	1432
....	62	SCIENCE		137	623
MUELLERG		NATURE	L65	205	1200

Example: 3 (Khanna)

Roe, Richard	*65*	J. Biol. Chem	....	6	103
Doe, J.		J. Cren. Bic	1969	7	55
Harrison, H.		J. Chem. Phy.	1970	47	1242
....	*72*	Science	....	147	623
Mullar II		Nature	175	210	1230

5.4.3 Source index

Source index part of Science Citation Index contains:

1. National bibliographic information about current citing articles included in the citation index part.
2. It is a complete author index of all items in source periodicals included in the Science Citation Index during a particular period.

3. Arrangement is alphabetical by the first citing author.
4. All co-authors are cross-referred to the first author.
5. For corporate work, there exists a separate section in the source index.
6. Corporate works are arranged alphabetically by the names of the organizations where the work was done.
7. Title, its volume, page, year of publication, and number of reference it has are also given besides citing author and collaborators.

In other words:

1. Source index is in effect a combined table of contents of all items in source journals in SCI during particular priod.
2. First author, joint author and title of the journal, its volume number, page number, year, type of documents code, number of references cited in it.
3. ISI accession number is followed by the full title of the article.

   It means each entry contained all the elements of information necessary in bibliographical reference.
4. Anonymous items included from source journals are arranged by the title of journals.
5. Since each entry is complete in itself this part can be used independently also to find out -

   Whether any contribution from a particular worker in a field has been reported in the current literature.

1. **Source Index** (one source of Index)

BOON JP (Author and Co-author)

DEGUENT	Vol. No.	Page	Pub. Year	No. of Ref.	Issue No.
PHYS	REV A 2	2542	70	36R	N6

TRANSPORT FUNCTION AND LIGHT SCATTERING IN SIMPLE DENSE FLUIDS (Full title)

---

2. **Source Index**

MUELLER DC INT BUS MACH
3165719 US 65 P 2R JAN12
MUELLER EG 'SEE' SMITH HL 3166263 US
MUELLER G CLAUS G SUBAC EA
NATURE 205 1200 65 L IOR N4977 62558
INTERPRETATION OF MICRO-STRUCTURES IN
CORBANACEOUS METEORITES

Explanation:

(1) Author G. Mueller with Collaborators G Claus and EA Subac

(2) Published in Nature 9, (3) Year 1965, (4) Page 1200, (5) Volume 65, (6) Number 4977, (7) References 10, (8) Full title, (9) Accession number (in ISI collection) 62558

5.5 Permuterm Subject Index

It was introduced in 1967. It is also called Permuted Term Subject Index.

5.5.1 Specific features

1. Every keyword of every citing article included in source index of a particular year are included in it.
2. Each title word related to every other title word in combination of pair of words.
3. It is in the natural language of the authors.
4. It is permuted so that every term used a title as a primary term and every two words combine.
5. With every other word in the title as a secondary term.

   One word with other word—Primary terms

   Two words with every other word—secondary term or co-term.

Permuterm Subject Index

APPLICATOR (1)	
BOTTLE (2)	ABUGHARE W (3)
CANCER	BATES (4)
CARTRIDGE	DELL MB
CUSTOM	AGR CHEM (5)
EXPERIENCE	
COLOUR SEE COLOR (6)	
....	
....	
MAGNESIUM	
SA MG (7)	

(1) = Primary term

(2) = Co-terms

(3) = Author

(4) = Articles need to be checked to cover all co-terms listed under the primary term

(5) = Journal title of the anonymous work

(6) = References of PSI spellings from the alternative one and

(7) = Related primary terms that should also be checked.

Computer is needed for the permutation of words in PSI.

Permuterm Subject Index (Prasan)

INTER STELLAR		
ATOMS	GREENEMBER	JM
BORON		DC
....		
....		
CLOUD S	CHAFFEE	FH
	COHEN	JG
	GOLDSTEI	JS
COLD	CROTCHER	RM

All the authors given below have used the word INTER STELLAR in the title of their papers in addition to the word shown opposite their names.

5.5.2 Steps in citation indexing

1. Deciding the coverage
2. Scanning of source documents
3. Preparation of entry
4. Sorting of entries
5. Consideration of entries
6. Arrangement
7. Preparation of indexes
8. Press copy marking

5.5.3 Merit of citation index

1. No more intellectual work is required in compilation.
2. It is mechanical work as it uses cited and citing documents.
3. It involves no terminology.
4. It does not involve artificial language.
5. It is not affected by new concepts.
6. It is a permanent feature to represent the document by its author, title, journal, etc.
7. It uses cross references to link the subjects with other related subjects.
8. Article from different areas are brought together.
9. It is easy to search the relevant materials from citation index then in other conventional index.
10. It helps in finding out core periodicals in the subject.
11. A citation index may reveal the genesis of a newly emerging subject.
12. Reading material is available in various physical forms.
13. It also reveals the scientists and authors in a particular field and also their contributions.

14. The author may know whether his contribution has been appreciated, and criticized.

5.5.4 Limitations

1. Citation Index does not satisfy the exhaustive approach of a user.
2. It does not specify the nature of relationship between cited and citing documents.
3. It does not provide conventional arrangement of logical subject arrangement.
4. A user should know at least one reference of a document on one subject.
5. Some highly important document may be left to be included in index.

Abstracting

6

During 19th century, abstract was considered as one of the most important public usages to cope with the continuous growth of various forms of documents. Abstracting was conceived mainly as a method of disseminating information from one scientist to another scientist.

Abstracting is an intellectual and skillful work. Abstract acts as retrieval media and current awareness tool. Abstract is a brief statement of the essential content of the original form indication of the characteristics of the original accompanied by bibliographical details. Its purpose is to:

(a) draw attention to the information contained in the original;

(b) provide a basis for the user to select the best out of vast;

(c) summarise a publication or article along with bibliographical details to trace the article.

Some definitions of 'abstract', given by experts, are given below:

Allen Kent: "An abstract is a summary of a publication or article accompanied by an adequate bibliographical description to enable the publication or article to be traced".

Meman M. Weisma: "It is an announcement medium whose objective is to provide knowledge of and an ordered and logical access to new primary literature. It can serve as a tool for both input to and retrieval from the system's information store."

Robert L. Calluison: "It is a terse presentation in the author's own language, of all the points made in the same order as in the original piece of primary documentation information—that can be a book, a research report, a periodical article, a speech, the proceeding of a conference, an interview, etc."

Robert E. Maigell: "An abstract is a condensation that presents succinctly, the objectives, scope, findings and documents."

A. Hikhailov and R.S. Reiljarvski: "An abstract is a summary of a document specifying its nature as well as the techniques, finding, time and place of an investigation; it also indicates the objectives, and main theoretical premises of a study, supplies the pertinent figures, formulae, tables, charts, and diagrams and references in the abstract publication, as well as the author's name."

Wibred Ashworth: "An abstract is a precis of information (coupled, of course, with a relevance for tracing) and in its narrower sense now usually refers to the information contained in periodicals, in short pamphlets or serial publications. It is however very rarely a literal precis of the original nor is it equipment to author's summary which very often goes by the name of author's abstract whether an abstract is a summary a précis of the original remains undecided."

In view of the above definition we can say that an abstract is a summary of documents, it is an abbreviated, accurate representation of original document. It has a separate entity and fulfils the object of tracing the information.

6.1 Qualities of a Good Abstract

1. It provides complete information.
2. It should be precise, accurate, informational, and act of belief.
3. It represents original data which has never been presented before.
4. It should not include any criticism.
5. It should include negative results.
6. It should be brief but its clarity should not be ignored.
7. It should be written in the third person.

8. It is assumed that the readers have some primary knowledge of the subject.
9. It usually begins with subject unless it is from title.
10. It includes author's own view on the possibility of applying the results described in it.
11. It should have minimum document and the abstract.
12. It should include an index.
13. It should not be costly and should be within the reach of the user.
14. It should have good printing, binding.

6.2 Importance

1. It is used for communication of nascent micro thoughts.
2. It bears intensive class number.
3. It includes selective journals and also articles which are of immense value.
4. It includes indexes which help in tracing the required information.
5. It is arranged according to author or subject.
6. It guides the reader to select best out of the vast collection.
7. It saves the time of the reader.

6.3 Purpose of Abstract

1. *It promotes current awareness*

All social men having knowledge of a subject are always eager to read more and more. On the other hand the investigator is stragged by the findings and conclusions of thousands of other workers—conclusions which he cannot find time to grasp, much less remember as they appear. Abstract helps the scientists to keep up with latest readings/informations. Information given in the abstract is surrogated in condensed form. It is a tool by current awareness.

2. *Time saving*

As an abstract is an accurate presentation and it is abbreviated, reader traces his required information without losing any more time. Abstract also represents the contents of the documents which give precise information to the readers. The summary will result in net saving of time.

3. *Selection is facilitated*

Title and subjects are two bases of information to select the readings. But both cannot be effective tools unless properly scanned and précised in identified position. If they are, they can provide selection facilities. Title may be a poor guide and misleading. Titles are generally not to represent the thought contents properly. Index provides terms inherent in title and helps the reader to trace his document or information.

4. *Literature search*

Abstracts are aid to search. Search cannot be made effective unless abstract is available. There are thousands of journals with millions of articles. It is very difficult to trace the required reading material. There is continuous flow of scientific literature. Abstract is the only medium to search the reading which a user wants to consult. There are several unpublished reports which can be traced through abstract.

5. *Indexing is made effective through abstract*

Index is a list of micro-thoughts but it is ambiguous without the details of the article. The summary in indexing guides the reader to be aware of the suitability of the article.

6. *Language barrier*

There are about 80 languages in various countries of the world in which articles are published in journals and reports of Engg. and Science appear. Generally, the scientists/ technologists know two or three languages. But the abstracts cover more than 50 languages and are translated into English language or the language of the land. The original articles or reports are made available in the language of their choice.

7. *Review preparation*

Abstracts are of special help in the preparation of bibliographies and reviews. There may be language problem. Data can be extracted from abstracts for use the reviews more efficiently than from the original articles. Related abstracts can conveniently be assembled for preparing simple or annotated bibliographies.

Allen Kent's functions

1. Current awareness
2. Reference: Back files accumulated information which may be consulted when required.
3. Classifying: Important aspects of a record are decided before preparing abstract.

C.L. Bervier's function of abstract

1. Abstract removes language barrier. Translations are provided by the information centers to the scientists in the language of his choice.
2. Scientists select their papers through abstract.
3. Abstract serves as a means of selecting or identifying the source material which is worth reading.
4. Information abstracts substitute for the original literature in many cases.
5. Abstract groups them and arranges.
6. Retrospective searches are greatly aided by classic indexed abstracts.
7. Abstract provides indexes subject wise or author wise.

6.4 Difference between Abstract and Index

Abstract	Index
1. An abstract is added to index.	1. The index is the list of micro-thoughts without abstract.
2. Abstract provides the summary of the material.	2. Index locates the material.
3. Abstract is short: 50 to 150 words—indicates primary point, methodology, argument and conclusion.	3. Index has no summary and hence failed to make available the views about the thoughts.

Similarity

1. Both save time.
2. Both help in locating the material.

Abstract can be divided in to two parts—

1. Citation part.
2. Abstract proper.

Citation part cites the document which is abstracted. The document may be:

1. an article in a periodical.
2. a book or monograph.
3. a patent, a standard.
4. a paper in conference proceedings.

Abstract describes the document in citation in such a way that it becomes possible for the reader to identify and locate the document easily.

There have been some standards in citation formulated and applied by India and England. A library and information centre follows these standards of abstracting.

The second part is abstract proper. This part does not follow any standard. There are certain rules and principles followed by abstractors. An abstractor must have—

(a) Knowledge and the audience.
(b) Abstract should have an orientation according to the requirement of the audience.
(c) Preparing the abstract for the bulletin.

6.5 Stages of Abstracting

6.5.1 First stage

The abstract should be self-contained and reveal the essential features of the original article or work. The following are the factors:

1. The introductory portion after paper or document should be read carefully. It reveals the objectives of the author in writing the paper.

2. If the document contains an author's abstract it should be read and examined in the light of the information contained in the text.
3. The summary and conclusion are given at the end of the document which is read.
4. The text is then scanned for information on the methodology of the work, data, etc.

6.5.2 Second stage

In this stage work is to organize the ideas which are selected for abstract. It is arranged in a helpful sequence. The sequence will be as follows:

1. Purpose—Introductory statement should indicate the goal, objectives of the study. It should clear the reasons for which the paper or the document is written.
2. Methodology, techniques.
3. Result—Reading report by the author.
4. Conclusion, interpretation or significance of the results.
5. Abstract may contain specialized information.

6.5.3 Third stage

Abstracting is the third stage:

(a) It should be written in easy to read prose words. Phrases should be easy so that these may be grasped by users.

(b) It should be in condensed version.

(c) It should be concise and unambiguous.

(d) It should use short sentences.

(e) Jargon, abbreviations, symbols' and trade names of language should be used with discretion.

(f) It should follow consistency.

(g) It should follow maximum economy.

6.6 Types of Abstracts

There are many types of abstracts:

1. Indicative or Descriptive Abstract

2. Informative Abstract
3. Title or Expanded title
4. The Summary or Synopsis Abstract
5. Abstract with a slant
6. Pseudo Abstract
7. Graphic Abstract
8. Telegraphic Abstract
9. Statistical or Tabulator Abstract
10. Auto-Abstract
11. Extracts
    (a) Author prepared Abstract
    (b) Abstract prepared by the subject experts
    (c) Abstract prepared by Professional Abstractors

6.6.1 Indicative or descriptive abstracts

The main purpose of abstracting is to help the reader to trace his information for which method of condensation or subject identification is followed. Different abstracts fulfil different purposes depending on emphasis and focus. They also differ on the method of preparation.

The indicative abstract indicates very briefly the nature and scope of a document or what the document belongs. It cannot serve as a substitute of the original document. It indicates the clues about the contents information of a document.

Example: Bibliographies, Symposia, proceedings, handbooks, state-of-the-art reviews.

6.6.2 Informative abstracts

The informative abstract contains in an abridged form all the important findings or ideas contained in the original document. It serves as a substitute of the original for getting some information. The abstract keeps to length from 150 to 250 words. It contains principal ideas, method, arguments and data and avoids excess and detailed explanation. Such abstracts are helpful in retrieving information.

Example: Chemical abstract, Biological abstract

In other words informative abstract summarises the original. They are usually in active voice; to increase directness, there is use of the present tense.

6.6.3 Title or expanded title

Title is treated more informative. Scientists like it more and more to consult information under title. A good title is often sufficient to indicate to the reader to trace his document.

6.6.4 Summary or synopsis

It is similar to indicative abstract. It gives an outline of the whole of the work. There are a majority of authors who are asked to write a summary of their papers. Their summarises are taken for publishing in abstract.

6.6.5 Abstracting with a slant

Abstracts are prepared keeping in view the area of research, nature of users. It makes the abstract biased in outlook. Dr. Ranganathan has named such type of abstracts as "slant in Abstracting".

The present age is an age of inter-disciplinary research. One article or document may be consulted by the readers of two subjects. This makes overlap of materials in the abstracts which has worldwide publication.

Example: Chemical Abstract, Biological Abstract,
Physical Abstract.

6.6.6 Pseudo abstract

It was introduced by T.E.R. Singer. This abstract is of paper which has never been written. It originated from the practice of invited speaker before his paper is submitted by the professional association for publication.

These papers are delivered ex tempore and may never be reduced to full text.

6.6.7 Graphic abstract

There are disciplines where a precise language of communication is available. Such type of abstracts are used in the field of Chemistry.

Example: Chemical Abstract, Index
Chemicus

These abstracts make full use of this language. This has been named as Graphic Abstract.

6.6.8 Telegraphic abstracts

The abstracts which are published regularly have tried to facilitate computer search. Such abstracts are called telegraphic abstracts. They may sound like telegram. The main purpose is to prepare abstract for computerized searching. It is a detailed index to a graphic record which is composed of significant words selected from documents, code symbols (role indicators) and punctuation symbols.

6.6.9 Statistical or tabular abstract

This is an abstract of some specific subjects.

Example: Thermodynamical properties.

The emphasis is exclusively on the data. The abstract is a summary of the data presented in tabular form.

6.6.10 Auto-Abstracts

It is an expensive venture. Intellectual effort is involved in it. There are two types of work—Intellectual and the Mechanical. Above all, H. Pater Luhen suggested the use of computer to extract abstract from the text of the document. Extract is made of keywords they contain. Keywords are determined statistically by the frequency of their appearance in the title and headings, and by their position. Computer selects the keywords out of the words in the first sentence of the paragraph which represents the subject. They are generally high frequency words put in a sequence. This is auto-abstract which is a collection of the most informative sentences from the original document. Luhen enunciated two principles for the auto-abstract process:

(a) Word occurrence—It means that important items of the text are preferred by the author. Certain words are repeated.

(b) Word proximity—In a sentence physical nearness of the words is indicative related to ideas they represent.

6.7 Types of Abstractors

1. Author prepared abstract
2. Abstract prepared by subject experts
3. Abstract prepared by abstractors

Author prepared abstract is prepared by the author of the document or article. The quality of these abstracts varies. Generally, authors are not aware of the rules and principles of abstracting. Authors need training and proper and sufficient experience. Moreover, the author may be biased and may ignore the special aspects of the subject. Many authors are asked by the editors of the journals to prepare the abstract and submit with the original document or the article. The training to authors is not possible because of their scattered area, nature and specialities. Experience counts more which author does not have. The abstract prepared by the author in the light of the guidelines will be of good quality and can be used as such.

Subject experts also prepare abstracts in professional journals. Those who are trained in abstracting and are also subject experts in the field can write the best and quality abstracts. These abstracts are accurate, comprehensive and lucid. Subject experts should be trained and given proper guidelines on abstracting techniques.

Professional abstractors are always better and suitable for abstracting. Such abstractors are employed to handle work and in other languages. Their work is usually prompt and competent. But professionals are expensive and professional abstractors have many advantages, like:

(a) Control on time.
(b) Proper format and standards.
(c) Language efficiency.
(d) Accuracy.

6.8 Abstracting Periodicals

Abstracting service is given through abstracting periodicals. An abstracting periodical is a regular issue which is compiled regularly with a concise summary of articles, new research monographs and other primary sources like reports, patents and standards. Only specific articles of a subject (often in a very limited field) are included in the abstracting periodical. Abstracting periodical contains comprehensive indexes for easily accessible articles published in journals. It also includes the part of the book and a patent, etc.

Abstracting periodicals are published by learned organizations, institutions, societies, government bodies or agencies. There are also a few periodicals which are published by private organizations, independent publishers. A few industrial or business organizations publish abstracting journals strictly for the use of their clients. Such abstracting periodicals are published for limited area or users.

Review journals are also playing an important role of abstracting periodicals. They provide current literature with extensive references. They include survey articles reviewing state-of-the art technology in a particular field.

(a) Issued regularly at a certain interval, i.e. weekly, monthly, quarterly, half-yearly, annual.

(b) Entries are given in classified group and order.

(c) Each entry is serially arranged.

Abstracting Services

1. Abstracting periodicals serve as key in having access to world literature.
2. It limits the area of search considerably.
3. It serves as subject bibliographies in the nature of abstracting periodicals.
4. It provides the literature of many languages at one place.
5. It is difficult to scan the technological literature to suit each individual. Abstracts facilitate the selection of papers to be read.
6. It helps in the selection of data.
7. It saves time.
8. Retrospective searches are greatly aided by classified indexed abstracts.

9. It helps in maintaining accuracy in the selection of literature to be read or translated.
10. It helps in deciding whether the contents of the documents are such as they need to be read in full.
11. It removes the language barrier.
12. Abstract serves both as handy summaries of the important data published on the subject during the period and as bibliographic guides to the field.
13. Abstracting services are the suitable media for reference service specially in view of the brevity of their contents, in respect of enquiries related to the current literature.
14. Abstracts are valuable both to layman and specialist.

Computer Network

7

Developments in computer and telecommunications have thrown open new vistas for better library services. The telecommunication technology gave rise to computer communications. Computers and communications technology have given rise to Library Networks and thus resource sharing in which academic, public, or special libraries form a network wherein the services and also processes may be shared. The document that used to be delivered by mail, on interlibrary loan is now being converted to 'Electronic Mail'. Indian libraries are also adopting these technologies, which may be attributed to the constraints in budget, and in trained manpower, due to which the percentage of automated libraries are very few. Many of the Special Libraries in India are automated. The Government is also encouraging the use of computerized libraries in India as it is the only alternative to provide better library service to the community.

7.1 Network

When two or more libraries are engaged in a common system of information exchanges through communications it is a network. A network usually consists of formal institutional arrangements whereby materials, information and services are available to all potential users.

The network:

Facilitates monitoring of vital socio-economic projects.

Provides online retrieval and updation of information.

Makes possible optimum utilization of costly computer resources.

Helps in sharing latest software tools.

Facilitates dissemination of information.

Helps in exchange of messages.

Provides emergency communication system.

7.1.1 Network topology

The design of hardware component is called 'nodes'. When these nodes are linked, they form patterns that are called starlike topology. Network of libraries is, therefore, a formal association of libraries and information centres, having the same or interrelated services or objectives. The individual libraries act together as one organization, with set responsibilities required of all members.

7.2 Need for Networks

The following factors force library and information centres to form into networks:

(a) Access to timely, reliable, and precise information, which is crucial for the development activities of a nation, is possible.

(b) The world literature in all fields of knowledge can be scanned regularly and relevant information from the point of view of research workers and R&D personnel can be selected, processed, organized and supplied.

(c) The effects of financial constraints of the individual libraries and the increasing prices of the reading material, will not hamper access to information sources.

(d) More users can be served.

(e) Several libraries acting in coordination, can eliminate some purchasing and processing costs as well as avoid unnecessary documents.

(f) With the application of computer and communication technologies, access to international databases and information centers could be possible through networks.

(g) The expertise and the new techniques developed in library services and information handling can be fully utilized, far more than one library can offer, all alone.

(h) The networks are offered as a solution to bridge the gap between the available information, and the users of that information spread far and wide.

Characteristics of Library Networks:

(a) *Data*: Bibliographic records

(b) *Retrieval*: Author/title/number (subject)

(c) *Access*: Telecommunication network/private network/ hard wired network

(d) *Users*: Librarians/Public/Researchers.

7.3 Library Network

Online library network is a group of libraries linked together in a complete and communications system for the purpose of participating in a common system or services. Online library networking emerges as a speciality which requires knowledge of library and information science, computing, telecommunications, information technology, economics, marketing, business, public service administration and behavioural science.

7.4 Categories of Networks

Online library networks can be categorized by the types of services they provide.

(a) Search services provide multiple databases for online searching.

(b) Customised-service networks offer graphic and other files for users, to search and modify for their own use. These services have been developed for cataloguing, circulation and inter-library loan activities.

International Networks

S.No.	Network	Host Organisation	Features/Services
1.	LC (1969)	Library of Congress	Machine Readable Catalogue Cards
2.	OCLC (1971)	Online Computer Library Centre Ohio	Quick information retrieval by sharing & saving cataloguing costs to industrial libraries
3.	WLN (1972)	Washington Library Network, Washington State University	800 institutes are participating and sharing the resources
4.	SOLINET	South Eastern Library Network, Louisiana	10 states are participating in this network
5.	RLG (1974)	Research Library Group	Cooperative collection development, preservation, conservation, inter-library lending and acts as research libraries Info network
6.	EURONET (1979)/DIANET (1980)	European Economic Community	Access to large number of databases, & resource among member countries of European Economic Community
7.	SCANNET (1976)	Scandinavian Council for Applied Research	Scientific Info & Doc. Network with nodes at Copenhagen, Gottenburg, Helsinki, Oslo, and Stockholm, 250 orgn use this facility
8.	TELENET	Bolt Barmark & Newman USA	Online network with access to SDC and Lockheed Databases in European Countries
9.	TIMENET (1977)	Tymeshare Inc USA	World's largest data carrying network with 650 micro-computers connecting 220 host computers

Subject Oriented Information Networks

S.No.	Network	Host Organisation	Features/Services
1.	MEDLINE	National Library of Medicine USA	Batch processed database on Medical Services
2.	AGRICOLA	Agriculture Online National Agricultural Library	Access to the needs of agricultural clientele
3.	INFOTERRA	International Referral Service for Sources of Information on Environmental issues World Centre, Nairobi	Referral service on sources of Info on Environmental problems
4.	ICDET	International Co-operation in the field of Transport Economic Documentation OECD	Document delivery system in UK along with 109 cooperating countries
5.	IRRD	International Road Research Documentation System OECD	Cooperative database building by 119 member countries
6.	IAEA	International Atomic Energy Agency	Information on Nuclear & Atomic Energy, 60 countries participate in this network
7.	ESA/IRS (1973)	European Space Agency/Information Retrieval System	Online Information retrieval services
8.	INIS	International Nuclear Information System IAEA, Vienna	Access to INIS index
9.	ERIC (1966)	Educational Resource Information Centre	Dissertation Abstracts of Masters & PhD. Theses in the field of Education, Humanities and Sciences
10.	Eurydice (1980)		Supplies information on Educational matters to policy-makers

S.No.	Network	Host Organisation	Features/Services
11.	APINMAP	Asia & Pacific Info Network on Medicinal and Aromatic Plants	Information services on Medicinal & Aromatic Plants. 13 Member countries use the facility
12.	IFIS	International Food Information Services	Information retrieval to Food Sciences Database
13.	ASTINFO (1983)	Rational network for exchange of Information in Sc. & Tech. in Asia & Pacific.	Consists of National Centers for Regional Information Services & associated countries

Indian Networks

S.No.	Network	Setting up Body	Service & Functioning
1.	NICNET	National Informatics Centre, Planning Commission, New Delhi	Provides computing & communication infrastructure to aid planning & monitoring the decision-making activities, facilitates flow of Info among 32 state and 439 district nodes. Evolved as an MIS to cater to the needs of Govt Deptts and agencies
2.	INDONET	CMC Limited, Hyderabad	Commercial Computer Network, designed for intra city communication of data transmission. It operates in a star network with control point at Delhi, using packet switching technology.
3.	VIKRAM	Department of Tele Communication, Govt. of India	Consists of 8 switching nodes & 12 remote access points with its centre at New Delhi

S.No.	Network	Setting up Body	Service & Functioning
4.	PSDN (1986)	Packet Switched data Network; Dept of Tele Communications	3 nodes network providing message transfer

7.5 Information Retrieval Network

Characteristics of Information Networks:

(a) *Data*: Bibliographic records (text numeric)

(b) *Retrieval*: Subject based (Boolean/key)

(c) *Access*: Telecommunication networks, private networks/ hardwired network

(d) *Users*: Intermediaries (End-users)

Information retrieval networks contain more bibliographic records. Retrieval is based largely on Boolean searching, besides other approaches. Thus, IR networks have varying type of data, Unstable user base, and Mix of professional/non-professional needs.

National Network

INFLIBNET Network

NICNET Network

INDONET Network

ERNET Network

INFOTEL Network

7.5.1 INFLIBNET

Information library network (INFLIBNET) is a programme of the University Grants Commission and was launched in May 1991. The main aim of INFLIBNET is to establish a national computer-communication network to link libraries and information centers in universities, colleges, UGC information centers, institutions of national importance, and R&D institutions. It will facilitate pooling, sharing and optimization of scarce library resources. It will help to modernize libraries and information centers in the country.

Services

(a) *Catalogue-based services*—Shared cataloguing of monographs, serial and non-book materials, Online catalogue access for shared cataloguing and location identification.

(b) *Data-based services*—Bibliographic databases services, retrospective search, SDI, Current awareness services.

(c) *Document supply services*—Inter-library loan request processing, Document delivery (Fax/non-fax).

(d) *Collection development*—Acquisition and assistance in selection and procurement.

(e) *Communication-based services*—Electronic Mail, Transfer/receiver messages, Bulletin board-view/updata bulletin board.

7.5.2 EARNET

EARNET is a mail service established by Department of Electronics during seventh plan (1986-90) to provide academic and research institutions with electronic mail facility. It is currently used by DSIR labs, Research centers and Academic institutions.

7.5.3 INFOTEL network

Like INDONET, INFOTEL network was established by "Informatics India Ltd." in 1989. It is an online service centre, with access to 1,500 International databases, tapped through DIALOG or EASYNET.

7.5.4 Regional networks

CALIBNET

The first Calcutta Library Network 'CALIBNET' was conceived in 1986. It is largely Govt. funded, and a sum of about 150 lakhs has already been invested by NISSAT, under Dept of Scientific & Industrial Research.

Objectives

CALIBNET stands for significantly improving resource utilization and service levels to patrons at individual libraries, providing automation facilities in:

1. Acquisition and fund accounting
2. Serials control
3. Cataloguing
4. Circulation
5. User services

DELNET

It was registered as a society in 1992. Since then, it has established an Electronic Mail Service among a few libraries for exchanging messages regarding current subscription, inter-library lending through the development of a union catalogue, etc.

DELNET provides automation facilities in:

1. Acquisition and fund accounting
2. Serial Control
3. Books and journals maintenance
4. Circulation
5. User service
6. Creation and maintenance of a bibliographic database
7. Interlibrary user services
8. Document copy and transfer facilities
9. Access to national and international databases
10. Union catalogue
11. Current awareness and SDI
12. Authority data
13. Subject profile
14. Abstracts

MALIBNET

Madras Library Network (MALIBNET) has been conceived by academicians, scientists and technologists of Madras to overcome the resource crunch in libraries, in and around Madras, and provide information at a low cost to the users. MALIBNET was installed and made operational in May 1993 with no direct funding from the Government. Currently six major academic institutions are directly linked to MALIBNET host system.

Services of MALIBNET

MALIBNET offers the following information services:

- Current serials acquired in about 50 libraries.
- Full journal holding of about 50 libraries.
- Contents information of about 400 important journals.
- Specialized database giving abstracts of articles.
- Electronic mail including international connectivity.
- Door delivery system, for document photocopies.

System Configuration

The architecture of MALIBNET has a central network service (NSC) located at INSDOC regional centre, Madras. The NSC houses the main computer which is a INTEL 486 based system with 32 megabytes of main memory, 1.2 Gigabytes of disc storage, x.25 networking interface, 16 ports modern communication, UNIX operating system and SYBASE.

Online Learning: Web-based Study

8

Motivation is the key to learning. Learner knows the reason of his satisfaction from the learning as he uses the knowledge. Learning happens more by experience than through mere instruction. Learning is more effective where the outcome involves the ability to do rather than the ability to talk about something. It is proved by the experiments that through direct learning, the learner learns and retains more than through the vicarious learning. Since learning is functional, the concepts and tools are acquired in view to be able to solve the problems.

Academicians had made researches to create different kinds of learning environment and the findings of these cognitive science researches have influenced the learning.

8.1 The Contents

Learning is the prime constitutent of learning environment. The contents contained under the topic focus exclusively on the concepts, facts and procedures of the subject. However, to operate the content effectively in any setting, learners also require:

(a) *Learning Strategies*: Which means knowing how to learn—explaining new fields, acquiring more knowledge in a familiar subject and reconfiguring knowledge already possessed are its main features.

(b) *Teaching Methods*: Another component of learning environment is the teaching methods which should provide the learner an opportunity to observe, interact, involve in and to explore expert strategies in the context of the subject to be learnt. The teaching methods should encourage and enhance the exploration capability and independence in learner.

This requires a sequence of increasing complex tasks, increasingly diverse problem-solving situations and the staging of learning. The content to be learnt should be organized in some optimal form so that it can be managed and grasped by the learner, whatever be his development stage or ability level. Learning is a social activity, therefore, the learning environment should have the technological, social and motivational characteristics of real world situations. It is only through encountering the subject knowledge in context that most students will learn when, where and how the knowledge applies in other situations. Therefore, special emphasis has to be laid on the way instruction is delivered, i.e. the instructional design.

8.2 Internet

The internet is fastly emerging as one of the most important tools which is speedy and most economical device to deliver bulk of information throughout the world. The world wide web (www or web), is the easiest and most popular way to access the internet. The web has also emerged as a recent mode of instruction. The web designers, educationists and cognitive psychologists, scientists are looking forward to how the instruction can be organized and presented effectively through web pages.

The web is a delivery medium, content provider and subject matter all in one. Using the web, teachers and designers can create instructional delivery mechanisms to guide their learners. These instructional delivery mechanisms or Web-based Training (WBT) are a collection of instructionally sound and well-designed web pages.

8.3 WBT: Online Learning

Web pages use multimedia (MM) elements to communicate the information as compared to heavily loaded abstract lectures. With the use of multimedia, the communication becomes more attention-attracting, clear, lively and interesting. The enquiry-discovery model used in internet instruction succeeded in creating interest and enthusiasm among learners to gain the knowledge through self-paced learning to the extent they want. The following may be the main features of web-based technology:

- One can access course material through internet/CD (web instruction emulated on CD).
- CD based video support.
- Tutor support to users through internet.
- Contact programmes may be organized at a few identified study centers to give support for complicated content/subject.
- Web access through dial up connections, Internet, Cable modems, etc. can be used.
- Learners can send their queries to the tutor through internet.

8.4 What is Web

The web uses text, graphics, interactively and to extending to video & audio. According to Raiser & Games' media selection diagramme (1983) and Merrill and Goodman's strategy and media selection technique (1972), these characteristics make the web most useful when used to explore intellectual and verbal knowledge and to a lesser extent when exploring effective learning with its versatility and interconnectedness.

8.5 The Instructional System Design (ISD) Model

This model primarily requires that learners meet a list of entry behaviours. They take little account of individual differences in learning and the differences in their prior knowledge and motivation. They define the final goals of learning in terms of behavioural changes that means, for them, it is more important to consider what the learners will be able to do or exhibit the required behaviour but not in terms what the learner has understood or learnt. This model is appropriate when the knowledge is procedural and can be exhibited.

8.6 The Hyper Media Design (HMD) Model

The HMD model defines how the learning environment and methods are organized and designs the knowledge that the designer hopes will be attained by the learner. Hyper media model is designed giving paramount emphasis to learner's objectives and providing guidance to help the learner for achieving these objectives. This model deals mostly with the pursuit of intermediate and expert knowledge in complex and ill-structured learning domains. In case the learning domain is simple or well-structured, then the use of ISD model is more considerable as compared to this HMD model.

8.7 What Helps to Design Good WBT

Following may be some simple steps that can be used to ensure the maximum utility of the WBT for learners:

(a) Establish formal development process primarily to meet the user needs.

(b) The rational choices of media types & technologies provide ample opportunities for intellectual interaction with the information which not merely includes many click areas.

(c) Keep in mind the individual differences in learning.

(d) Linear thinking & design should be avoided. The user decides the direction best suited to him/her for achieving their set learning goals.

(e) Readability of material on the screen is an important area of concern for users. Too much scrolling should be avoided.

(f) In WBT design, avoid useless information and design the course material with a view that the user wants to learn something of value and get the satisfaction for the money and time the user spends.

CD-ROM

9

Rewritable magnetic media such as floppy disk, hard disk and tape are familiar to almost all users of technology. Both removable and compact, floppy disk provides a vehicle for distributing programs and data. The often non-removable hard disk supports random access for large amounts of data, typically starting at around a meagre 20 Mbytes Disk drives supporting hundreds of Mbytes are proliferating, and drives in the Giga byte (1.024 Mbytes) range are commercially available. Magnetic tape provides a cost-effective means of storing large amounts of data where random access is not required; for example, data backup, for archive purposes, and for submission of CD-ROM data to replication companies. Used to back up hard disks, tape streamers offer a safety net in the event of a catastrophic system failure. Subsequent data recovery simply involves reading the tape contents back to a functioning hard disk.

A read-only digital storage medium (DSM), CD-ROM supports up to about 660 Mbytes data storage capacity in standard form. It offers numerous features unrivalled by current magnetic media, including vast storage capacity, compactness of design, reliability and durability.

Grolier's Academic American Encyclopedia was first published on CD-ROM in 1985. Twenty volumes consisting of 9,000,000 words or 10,000 pages, consumes a mere fifth of the data capacity of one 12cm diameter disc! The 1990 edition of Grolier's Encyclopedia included full colour photographs for the first time. Many encyclopedias on CD-ROM are cheaper than their paper equivalent.

CD-ROMs are the largest data memories available for commercial PC applications. They are, unlike 'hard disks', very light, small in size, and easy to transport. In modern times most of the CD-ROMs are large size textual databases such as reference books, trade directories, catalogues, bibliographies, indexing and abstracting periodicals, full text journals, bibliographical databases, etc. Moreover, the present version CD-ROMs have integrated the text with graphics, sound and pictures, which has resulted in becoming more interactive information systems. When CD-ROM is connected with networks, the resulting CD-ROM Networking would be much more effective. CD-ROM networking offers an opportunity to make vast amounts of data/information available simultaneously and provides greater speed and independence.[1]

CD-ROM was introduced in 1985. It is one of the derivatives of compact audio disk. According to the Optical Publishing Association report, in 1988 the CD-ROM application's revenue went up to $ 280 million. But in the next year itself, the revenue growth went up to approximately 138%, i.e. $ 665 millions. The disk is normally made out of polycarbonate, in between two layers there will be a metallic film on which the actual data will be recorded in a 'pitted language'. For the present, all the CD-ROMs are single side recorded disks and the efforts for both sides recording are still going on. Reading is done by a non-contact method which is free of wear.

It is important to note that non-contact allows the fast random access in data storage and retrieval. The CD-ROM has become one of the best powerful tools for storing and retrieving of huge amount of information in libraries and information centers. CD-ROM is an inexpensive medium and could distribute a large amount of information very easily. In addition it supplements other media.

Advantages

(a) High storage capacity.

(b) Fast and random access of information.

(c) Very low publishing cost.

(d) Easy to distribute.

(e) High data integrity.
(f) More durability.
(g) High archival life.
(h) More reliable.
(i) Effective standardisation.
(j) More resistant to damage.
(k) Easy to use.

Disadvantages

(a) Since it is read only in memory, one cannot write, store or alter the data after mastering.
(b) A CD-ROM workstation could run only one application at a time.
(c) The equipment and production is too expensive.
(d) Careless use of disks causes not only damage to disks, but also leads to incorrect reading of data.
(e) It is user-friendly but a minimum basic training or knowledge is required to use.
(f) Lack of market stability.

Suitable for libraries

(a) It saves high cost building and shelf storage space.
(b) Unlike Online databases, the users themselves can do their information searches, which gives more satisfaction.
(c) Involves least cost if compared to hard copies.

9.1 Optical Disk Storage

In the form of videodisks or compact disks (CDs), optical disks represent a new trend in small, high-capacity storage of images and sound. A single optical disk stores nearly 1 GB of data on one side. To put this storage capacity into perspective, an optical disk can hold 800 television quality images or 60 minutes of high fidelity music. New storage technologies using optical disks exceed the storage capacities currently available with magnetic disks of the same size. Optical disks differ from magnetic disk storage by the way data is stored and read from the storage media. A laser beam is used to write and read data on these reflective disks, so they are also known as laser disks. In this technology a laser hits a layer of metallic material spread over the surface of a disk. When data is being entered, heat from the laser produces tiny spots on the disk surface. To read the data, the laser scans the disk, and a lens picks up different light reflections from the various spots. Optical disks are less sensitive to environmental fluctuations, and they provide more direct-access storage at a cost that is much less per Megabyte of storage than the magnetic disk alternative.

- read-only
- recordable, and
- erasable

9.2 Read-Only Disks: CD-ROM

In C.D. recording, the analog sounds of music are translated into their digital equivalents and stored on a 5.25 inches optical disk. In effect, anything that can be digitized can be stored on optical disk like data, text, voice, still pictures, music, graphics, and video.

CD-ROM (Compact Disk—Read Only Memory) is an audio CD technology and is created at a mastering facility, just as audio CDs are created at a recording studio. The ideal way is to distribute large amounts of data, such as an online encyclopedia or multimedia presentations. Computer programs and associated user manuals are distributed on CD-ROM video sequences. CD-ROM drive is nearly devoid of buttons and LCD readouts, except for a button to load and unload a disk and a few lights to tell you when the drive is reading a disk or playing music. The drive is controlled by a software in your PC that sends instructions to controller circuitry that is either a part of the computer's motherboard or on a separate board installed in an expansion slot. CD-ROM drive performance provided faster access speeds. The original single-speed 150 KBps CD-ROM drives are now quite obsolete. Double-speed 2x(300 KBps) and quad-speed 4x(600 Kbps) CD-ROM drives currently offer the best performance for the price, with access speeds at 300 msec or less. Faster drives, viz. 6x and 8x(1.2 MBps) are on the drawing board multimedia disks. The most demanding CD-ROMs of all are written only for 2x or 4x drives.

Optical storage techniques make use of the pinpoint precision possible with laser beams. Optical storage devices focus a laser beam on the recording medium, which is a spinning disk, same as phonograph record. Some areas of the disk reflect the laser light into a sensor (called lands), whereas others scatter the light (called pits). As the disk rotates past the laser and sensor, a spot that reflects the laser beam into the sensor is interpreted as a 1 and the absence of a reflection as a 0. A laser can read an optical disk surface, where pitted areas represent binary 0's and landed areas represent binary 1s.

9.3 CD-ROM (Compact Disk-Read-Only Memory)

CD-ROM uses the same technology that is used in music CDs. If we have a sound board and speakers connected to our computer, we can play CDs with our PC.

CD-ROM has a high precision and data density and a single CD can typically hold up to 660 MB of data. Its diameter is 5.25 inches (12cm disk). No one can change the data on CDs therefore CDs are the distribution medium of choice. A CD is a thin layer of aluminium sandwiched between two layers of plastic. The aluminium has a spiral track that contains millions of tiny pits (1s). As the CD spins a laser beam shines on the track. To manage the enormous data files on CD-ROMs we use special indexing methods. The indexes on CD-ROMs contain information on how to find virtually every single word on the CD-ROM.

Computers with CD-ROMs can display graphics with quality as high as that we see on television.

However, it is costly and CD drives are still slow. A drive that meets the multimedia PC4 standard for performance only has to move 1100KB of data per second. A good hard drive, by comparison, transfers 40 MB of data per second. Whereas on time scale the internal hard drive can find the data when your application asks for in 10 msec, and on the other side CD-ROM drive takes upto 500 msec for the same task. The other reason is that you cannot write to portions of a writable CD-ROM that already have data written to them. You can't delete or change what is already there.

A standard has been evolved for recording information on CD-ROM. The standard used is called ISO-9660.

9.3.1 Recordable Disk: Write Once, Read Many (WORM)

WORM is an ideal medium for making a permanent record of data, i.e. it can be a feasible alternative to magnetic tape for archival storage.

Example:

(a) Many banks use WORM disks to store a record of each day's transactions. The transactions are written to an optical disk and become a permanent record that can be read but never altered.

(b) Another popular application of WORM disks is in information systems, that require the merging of text and images that do not change for a period of time.

9.3.2 Erasable Disks: Magneto-Optical Disks

A hybrid disk, called magneto-optical (MO), combines the best features of magnetic and optical disk technologies. A magneto-optical disk has the high-volume capacity of an optical disk but can be written over as a magnetic disk. The disk surface is coated with plastic and embedded with magnetically sensitive metallic crystals. To write data, a laser beam melts a tiny spot on the plastic surface and a magnet aligns the crystal before the plastic coils. The crystals are placed in such a way that some reflect lights and others do not. Later on, when the data is read by a laser beam, only the crystals that reflect light are picked up.

But these magneto-optical disks are too expensive and do not offer anywhere near the kind of reliability that users have come to expect of magnetic media. The access time in magneto-optical disks are relatively slow, about the same as a low-end Winchester disk.

9.4 Applications of CD-ROM

CD-ROM provides instantaneous reference service to their users. All the prominent libraries in the developed countries have already started using them effectively, in providing various types of services to their users.[2]

(i) *Library Automation*: There are a number of commercial cataloguing tools available on CD-ROM in the market which are useful both for retrospective and new cataloguing. There are a few CD-ROM-based serial controls also.

(ii) *Library Catalogues*: British Library, Library of Congress OCLC, etc. have started the distribution of their catalogue on CD-ROMs.

(iii) *Books and Serials Acquisition*: Almost all the international publishers in print version, have started publishing on CD-ROMs, e.g., RR Bowkers' Books-in-print, Whitakers, British books in print, etc. on CD-ROM.

(iv) *Reference Work*: There are so many reference tools like encyclopedias, dictionaries, directories, mapping services, technical reference manuals, year books, etc. available on CD-ROM.

(v) *Databases*: Two types of databases are available on CD-ROM: Full text databases, such as 'Computer Library, 120 publications and presently having 43000 articles on CD-ROM. The second and more popularly available databases on CD-ROM are indexing and abstracting publications. There are many Online database publishers who have started publishing their databases in science and technology, engineering, computing, earth sciences, medicine, agriculture, food sciences, library science, etc. on CD-ROM, e.g. Dialog on disc in various subjects, NTIS discs, LISA, Engineering Index, etc.

9.5 Networking

The CD-ROMs are very much economical and useful in any organization where the same data or database or program is required by a number of users. Linking of several workstations in a LAN is made possible to all the users, to access the information from all other systems in the network. It also makes possible to link multiple CD-ROM drives to a single workstation, which is again connected to LAN for the access of number of users.[3]

9.5.1 CD-ROM drives

Though little appears to separate drives on the surface, deeper analysis reveals many subtle differences that govern overall performance. Buffer size helps improve speed of operation by permitting the drive to search for and read data without waiting for the computer to accept all outgoing data. The buffer is simply an area of RAM (Random Access Memory) which acts as a temporary store between drive and computer. Buffer sizes of 64 Kbytes are common.

Average access time, a measure of how long it takes the laser head to locate and begin reading an appropriate region of disc, is measured in milliseconds (ms), and tends to vary from 1500 ms down to 300 ms. Integral to access time, latency represents time taken for the read head to find the appropriate CD-ROM data block during random access. This tends to increase with turns of track farthest from the disc's center. Typically, latency may vary from between 50 and 80 ms for innermost turns, and approximate 150 ms for outermost turns.

Average data transfer rates vary little and can be assumed to be fixed at either 150 Kbytes/sec or 171 Kbytes/sec. Data capacities vary little also, and using standard technology a maximum of around 660 Mbytes can be achieved. As far as the average user is concerned, data capacity is not a function of drive architecture but of the disc itself; size of data blocks and play time dictate data storage capacity.

CD-ROM data blocks provide a means of storing information logically to yield a data structure which is both manageable and readable. Using one-hour discs, the two different user data block sizes of 2 Kbytes and 2.28 Kbytes in Mode 1 and Mode 2 operation, give 553 Mbytes and 602 Mbytes data capacities, respectively. All high specification drives support Mode 1 and Mode 2 operation, including that integrated into the CDTV.[4]

A less important area of difference concerns the maximum data transfer rate, which tends to be noticeably higher than the average. In fact, it can be more than four times greater. Maximum data transfer rate is achieved through burst transfer (or burst mode), where the drive seizes the computer processor time completely. However, it cannot be sustained for reasonable periods of time.

High specification drives can read discs encoded according to High Sierra Group (HSG) and ISO 9660 formats, both of which concern the storage of alphanumeric data. All but an extreme minority cope with these, and also double as audio CD players. Note, contrary to many articles which state categorically that High Sierra is the same as ISO 9660, there are subtle differences. For example, High Sierra drives have existed which are unable to play some ISO-9660 discs. The incompatibility is a function of software and, in particular, the MS-DOS CD-ROM extensions which were initially designed to the High Sierra standard but nowadays conform to ISO 9660.

Other optical disc formats include Philips Compact Disc-Interactive (CD-1) and the Apple Hierarchical Filing System (HFS). However, ISO currently remains most widespread, and can be seen in multimedia through Commodore CDTV.

9.5.2 CD-ROM drive installation

Almost all desktop computers are designed with a view to future expansion, able to accommodate extra floppy disk drives, hard drives, fax cards, network cards, and the many other population peripherals. IBM PC XT, ATs and PS/2, for example, include a number of expansion slots intended to accommodate such add-ons. The Macintosh is also expandable, with the II series a little more so than the Macintosh SE and Classic. However, external embellishments can always be accommodated due to the incorporation of a small Computer System Interface (SCSI) on all Macintosh computers, which began with the Macintosh Plus.

CD-ROM drives can be either internal or external. Portable drives such as the NEC CDR-35 and Philips CM50 generally provide an inexpensive route to CD-ROM.

Other than saving desk space and often reducing the number of mains leads, there are no other advantages in using internal drives. Lack of space or an insufficient power supply can force the need for an external or portable drive. Indeed a number of desktop computers on the market support little more than two 3.5" drive bays, as it seems that the advent of surface mount technology has encouraged some manufacturers to opt for yet smaller cases than ever before. Apple and Tandy led the trend towards small footprint computers, but IBM was the catalyst with its PS/2 range.

Insofar as the PC is concerned, problems of small cases could be overcome using 'CD-ROM cards', which like hard cards would embody a drive mechanism and controller as a single module. However, standard 12cm CD-ROM drives would be too large for many machines. Internal or external, the connection of a CD-ROM drive requires an appropriate interface, of which there are basically two kinds: proprietary bus interface and SCSI.

The simplest interfaces are indigenous to particular drives, and include a proprietary bus connection. This means that a PC XT/AT machine requires a different interface card from a PS/2 system or compatible. Similarly, neither of these interfaces suit Apple computers, which require SCSI compatible drives. Proprietary bus interfaces are indigenous to different manufacturers, resulting in zero interchangeability between different drives. For example, you cannot simply swap between Hitachi and NEC drives.

Uptil 1991 all proprietary bus connections took place over an eight-bit bus, giving compatibility across the board in terms of PC XTs and ATs. For PS/2s and compatible systems, all of which possess the Micro Channel Architecture (MCA) bus, an appropriate MCA interface card is required. SCSI is now universal and officially backed by ANSI (American National Standards Institute). Aimed to provide interchangeability between peripherals and computer systems from different manufacturers, it is not intended solely for the attachment of CD-ROM drives. It is often used to interface hard disk drives, printers and other peripherals. In fact, more and more devices now come with SCSI interfaces. However, SCSI is a vague standard, and you should exercise caution when making assumptions with regard to interchangeability.

SCSI implementations tend to vary in performance in terms of speed of input and output operations. For example, some controllers consist of the most basic bidirectional bus, offering low data transfer speed, and in many instances they barely meet official SCSI requirements. SCSI controller cards can be fitted to PX XT/AT machines and PS/2s (and compatibles), where 'suitable' SCSI drives (or compatible peripherals) can then be connected. Controller cards for PC XT/ATs and PS/2s permit the connection of seven peripherals and cost around $250. (Check your system or manual for the existence of such a card).

The main advantage of a SCSI drive is interchangeability where, for example, it can be disconnected from an IBM PC or compatible machine and simply added to an Apple Macintosh. For this to be so, you will need appropriate drivers and interface adapters.

9.5.3 Category of drives[5]

CD-ROM drives are of three types. (1) Peer-to-peer networking, (2) Client-server-networking, and (3) Operating System-based networking.

1. *Peer-to-peer CD-ROM drives networking*

In peer-to-peer networking CD-ROM drives are connected to one of the computers on the network (Figure 1). After connecting, the CD-ROM drive will be given a letter (e.g. E: or F:) through which the other computers can be used to scan all the attached drives.

This drives networking is:

(a) Inexpensive and easy to install the drives.

(b) One CD-ROM drive will serve the requirements of several users.

But—

(a) Access to the CD-ROM is slower.

(b) 10 users is the maximum limit to get satisfactory results in this network.

2. *Client-server networking*

The CD-ROM drive can be attached to the network in two ways: (i) to the file server, and (ii) dedicated CD-ROM server. First approach is the simplest as the drive is attached to the server with an SCSI host adaptor. Second way is to create a totally dedicated CD-ROM server (Figure 2) with attached CD-ROM drive(s).

It has the following advantages:

(a) It allows the users to connect to CD-ROM at the same time;

(b) It allows to combine CD-ROM 'Juke box' servers;

(c) File server is dedicated to the function of sharing data.

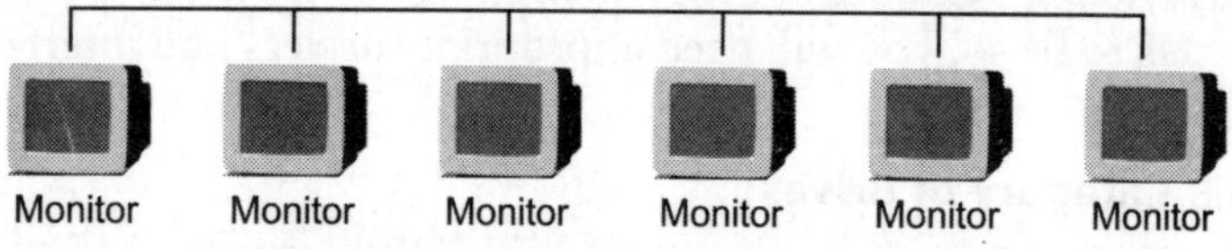

Figure 1: Peer-to-peer CD-ROM drives network

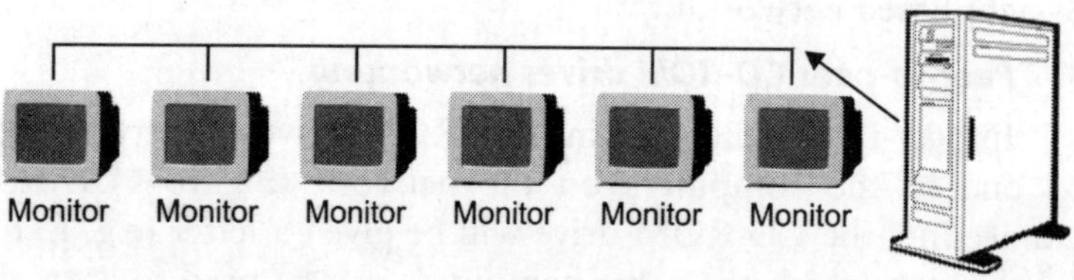

Figure 2: Client-server CD-ROM network

9.6 CD-ROM Operation

The underlying technology of CD-ROM is markedly similar to that used in Philips' first optical video disc system demonstrated in Eindhoven as early as 1972. This research and development led to LaserVision. CD-ROM is a reflective light system, where laser light is shown against turns of track which are encoded with digital data using pits and areas of land. Pits scatter the laser light, while areas of land produce reflected light. Reflected light is diverted to a photodetector that produces a series of electrical pulses corresponding to encoded data.

A CD-ROM disc rotates a speed to provide a constant average read rate of around 75 block/sec. Because data is embedded in the track (or tracks) of a CD-ROM at a uniform density (which equates to 0.6* 10 bits/mm2), the disc must spin faster when the read head converges on its center (or vice versa). This is quite unlike traditional vinyl audio discs which rotate at a constant angular velocity (CAV). The required constant linear velocity (CLV) is achieved by coordinating the position of the read head with speed of rotation using a simple feedback system.

The reason why standard drives operate in CLV mode rests firmly with the manner in which discs are encoded. It would have been equally possible to vary the distance between pits on a CD-ROM and so adopt a CAV system.[6] There is a reasonable argument to suggest that CAV would have eliminated the need to vary motor speed and so reduce drive prices. It would also have reduced access times. However, experience of Philips LaserVision (videodisc) player indicates that almost twice as much data can be stored on a CLV disc.

Like all random-access, storage devices, encoded information has to be organized into manageable data blocks so that it may be located and retrieved. Irrespective of whether or not a disc uses one track or upto 99, CD-ROM data blocks of 2,352 bytes are used. The amount of user data that CD-ROM data blocks provide is a function of Mode of operation. A Mode 1 disc, for example, will yield just 2 Kbytes (2,048 bytes) user data, while Mode 2 capacitates 2.28 Kbytes. Tables 1 and 2 show the CD-ROM data block structure in Modes 1 and 2, respectively, Mode 1's lower user data is due to demands imposed to error detection and correction codes. Conventional CD-DA (Compact Disc-Digital Audio) data blocks comprise 2336 bytes of digital audio.

Table 1

Mode 1 Block Structure

Designation	Size	Byte Number
Synchronisation	12 bytes	0-11
Header	4 bytes	12-13
User Data	2,048 bytes	16-2,063
Error Detection	4 bytes	2,064-2,067
Space	8 bytes	2,068-2,075
Error Correction Code	276 bytes	2,076-2,351

Table 2

Mode 2 Block Structure

Designation	Size	Byte Number
Synchronisation	12 bytes	0-11
Header	4 bytes	12-15
User Data	2,376 bytes	16-2,351

The addition of error detection and correction codes makes Mode 1 discs more suited to data highly sensitive to error, such as computer software. In multimedia, Mode 2 is commonly used for the storage of video and audio data, as its accuracy is not so critical.

Like audio CD, each second of playback results in 75 blocks read irrespective of mode; thus, storage capacity is increased in Mode 2 as is the average data transfer rate. The average user data transfer rate of a disc can be calculated by applying the following simple formula:

Average user data transfer (Kbytes/sec) = block/sec* user block data (Kbytes)

Mode 1:

Average user data transfer rate = 75 * 2

= 150 Kbytes/sec

turning to Mode 2 discs, we have a noticeable improvement brought about through increased user block data:

Average user data transfer rate = 75 * 2.28
= 171 Kbytes/sec

Mode 2's percentage increase in user block data over Mode 1 is reflected in average data transfer rate. Hence, the significance of user block data.

It should be pointed out that 'data transfer rates' are quite different. Data sheets and drive specifications regularly opt for the former when they mean the latter. For example, in Mode 1, block data is significantly greater than user data largely because of the inclusion of error correction code (ECC).

9.6.1 CD-ROM addressing and user Data capacity

CD-ROM addressing is carried out using measurements of time and data blocks read, Minutes, Seconds and Blocks provide enough information to locate any item of information. (Note, these are inherited directly from CD-DA). For example, considering a one-hour CD-ROM, absolute addressing would take the following form:

Minutes (M) : 0—59
Seconds (S) : 0—59
Blocks (B) : 0—74

A track beginning mid-way through the CD-ROM, for instance, is addressed 29:29:37 (M:S:B).

The length of a CD-ROM in minutes and the data block size in terms of user data, can be used to calculate user data capacity with pinpoint accuracy. For example, consider the following simple formula:

User data capacity = disc length (seconds) *blocks read/ second * usable block data

Applying this formula to calculate the precise data capacity of a one-hour Mode 1 disc gives:

User data capacity = 3600 * 75 * 2,048 bytes
= 552,960,000 bytes
= 527 Mbytes

Similarly, the capacity of a one-hour Mode 2 disc:

User data capacity = 3600 * 75 * 2,336 bytes
= 630,720,000 bytes
= 602 Mbytes

User data capacity, besides being a function of user data block size, also depends upon disc play time. Though this can be up to about 79 minutes, the original Philips/Sony specification embodied a 60-minute play time.

Once again it is important to recognize the difference between 'data capacity' and 'user data capacity' of which the former will always be significantly larger, and even more so using a Mode 1 disc. Drive specification sheets consistently fail to differentiate between the two. It should be noted that, in most instances Mode 2 data blocks have to coexist with Mode 1 data blocks on the same disc. Such mixed mode discs are necessary where both software (retrieval system, for example) and video and audio are stored on the same disc. It can be assumed, therefore, that technically a solely Mode 2 disc is not possible.

9.6.2 Operating system-based networking

There are many operating systems, i.e. DOS, Windows and LAN OS which were not written with CD-ROM drives. A few companies like Microsoft have written an extension to DOS users, a super set of commands to enable a CD-ROM unit to be arrested as another hard disk. Microsoft also introduced Windows NT (New Technology) which has the ability to read CD-ROMs directly if they are attached to the computer via a drive. The new Netware, 'Netware Loadable Modules' (NLMs), allows a CD-ROM drive to work successfully.

Advantages

(a) It gives a very fast and better performance than peer-to-peer method,

(b) It does not require any additional software, other than networking software,

(c) It is the most effective way of attaching CD-ROM to a network.

Disadvantage

Due to extra burden on the file server, the time spent on core function may be reduced.

9.7 CD-ROM Networking Systems

There are five systems for running a CD-ROM network: (i) CD Net, (ii) LAN tastic, (iii) Opti-Net, (iv) Multi-Platter, and (v) Novell Netware.

9.7.1 CD Net system

Meridian Data, Inc USA introduced the first CD-ROM networking systems for standard Local Area Networks (LANs) in 1987. CD Net is primarily developed for a small to medium sized LANs which will provide a lot of facilities such as duplicate disk capabilities, making use of CD-ROMs on a network, as fast as, or even faster than, if they have their own CD-ROM disk drive. This system can be configured for Token Ring, Ethernet, Novell Netware, NetBios LANs, WANs. Each CE Net accommodates up to 28 CD-ROM drives (16 gigabytes) per system.

9.7.2 Lanstastic system

Artisoft's LAN stastic is cheaper, easy-to-install and use CD-ROM LAN system. It hardly takes 20 minutes for installation. It is an ideal network solution for a small library and a small CD-ROM network. It is advantageous because of its ability to share Microsoft MS-DOS Extensions. The extension need not be installed on each workstation. However, only on 'the server' the extension will work and allow a maximum of 120 users.[7]

9.7.3 OPTI-Net system

Introduced by Online Computer Systems Inc's OPTI-Net it is another CD-ROM LAN system which provides software and hardware options. It gives high performance access to CD-ROM database over any NetBIOS compatible network. There are three options (i) attaching dumb terminals to a host PC via Multi-DOS; (ii) adding CD-ROM to an existing network via OPTI-Net; and (iii) setting an independent and dedicated CD-ROM network such as CD Net. OPTI-Net can be configured for Novell's IPX/SPX and NFS (Network File System) users. This system comes as a package which includes a four-drive CD-ROM Jukebox unit, the OPTI-Net drive sharing software, adaptor card and cable. This system was rated by server reviewers of the magazines.

9.7.4 EZ-Net

EZ-Net offers total CD-ROM Network solutions. EZ-Net is a turnkey CD-ROM Network that can be installed and operated by the average person. It can be straightaway plugged in and install the CDs. The access time to any CD file ranges from 6-15 seconds. EZ-Net software provides fast access to CDs library, simultaneously by multiple users. Its operating system supports DOS, OS/2, Windows NT, Novell Netware, SCO UNIX, l Power LAN, SunSoft Solaris, UNIX DEC Pathworks, Banyan, IBM LAN server. It is an inexpensive system. It includes EZ-Station 1 (comprising 486DX-33 Processor, 4 MB RAM, 128K cache, 245 MB HDD, 3½" FDD, 2 Serial and parallel ports, 16 Bit 1 MB Video Windows Accelrator, Ethernet 10 Base-T, 16 Bit PIO SCSI Interface, 16 Bit Sound Blaster Card, 14" rate, 29/80W Stereo speakers, MS DOS 6.2 and EZ-MENU 4.5 SW, LAN drivers for multiple networks and Video drivers).

9.7.5 Multi-Platter system

Silver Platter, a database vendor, has developed the multi-user system called 'Multi-Platter' which can allow maximum 20 terminals within a distance of 600 feet from the workstation. It was installed at Boston College (USA) in Sept 1989. It has got the facility of searching the same disk simultaneously by different users and also eliminates the waiting time in a LAN. Presently it is having a dial-in capability for remote users and a bridging module which links Multi-Platter to a campuswide or other general network.[8]

It is useful because of the following:

(a) Since it is a modular system, one can add more drive towers to increase the storage capacity according to one's requirement.

(b) It provides statistics package, to help the management for monitoring which CD-ROM and workstation is used how long, etc. Usage statistical reports can be made daily, weekly, monthly or any block of time, for finding out the usage of CD-ROMs and workstation also.

(c) One can cut down a lot of expenditure, because one disk is shared by so many users.

(d) There is more user satisfaction.

9.7.6 Novell Netware systems

It was introduced by Phillips Interactive Media Systems. By adding a Networking Interface Card (NIC) and a driver software to the working station, all the work-stations in the network will function as dedicated CD-ROM system. The server software not only requests but also identifies the drive to be accessed and retrieves the information and passes back. A server can support a maximum of 100 concurrent users and eight CD-ROM drives. The data/information can be stored on the server's hard disk. By using with Ethernet, this system will accept the users within a distance of 2.5 kms. It also allows access by telephone/modem link within a distance of few hundred kms from the server.

9.7.7 LAN Software

(i) *CD Net LAN Software*: Meridian Data's CD-Net supports a variety of CD-ROM devices on LANs including Netware 3.11 (using a NLM) and on most NetBIOS LANs using a dedicated CD-ROM server. CD Net is licensed on a concurrent user basis to grow with application needs.

(ii) *CD Connection Software*: CD connection is a software that allows CD-ROM users to access multiple drives simultaneously over a LAN. It runs on Ethernet, ARCNET, Token Ring and other networking systems and provides networking capabilities to CD-ROM drives.

(iii) *SCSI Express 600 CDX*: SCSI Express is a software-based CD-ROM, sharing solutions which enable multiple devices to be integrated on a single SCSI host adopter. It runs on a shared file server but performs better from a dedicated system. It consists of several modules including support for WORM and CD-ROM. The latest module support ISO 9660 standard CD-ROM formats.

9.8 Optical Disk Technology

Optical disk technology has solved the problems of storing and retrieving of large amounts of data on a small optical disk, but they are for single user only. CD-ROM system allows that the user could manipulate a vast amount of data according to his needs. There are a few CD-ROM systems networked and shared by several users in the network. It has resulted in increase in cost. Therefore, CD-ROM technology is more economical than Online systems. By connecting all the optical disk systems together, the retrieving time can also be reduced enormously. Jukebox concept of optical disk library has been marketed and solved most of these problems. The number of disks and disk drives depend upon the requirement of the user, loading and unloading of disks will be done by a picker (robot) automatically within a few seconds.

Normally all the optical disk libraries will have four basic units: (1) Storage matrix, (2) Disk drives domain in which all the disk drives will be fitted at one place, (3) Robotic Picker, which will be used to pick up the disk according to the computer instructions, through the Controller, from the stack and put into the drive; after searching is over, it will automatically put the disk back in the stack from where it was picked, and (4) The Controller which is the main unit which will accept the commands from the computer and user, and get the searching done in the library. It is the central controlling unit which will be controlling rest of the three units in the library.

9.8.1 Jukebox systems

Voyager CD-ROM

The 'VOYAGER' CD-ROM library has been introduced whose maximum capacity is 175 Gigabytes. However, these systems have different storage capacities, depending upon the users' requirement, such as the number of CD-ROMs 90, 180, 270 CD-ROMs and also having the maximum facility for 8 half-height CD-ROM disk drives. It is the option of the user to choose the number of disks and drives. The Voyager disk library will be able to access the information within 300 milliseconds and its average disk transfer time is 5 seconds. Voyager is the first CD-ROM optical disk library, which is particularly suitable for library applications. It is very much useful and cost-effective for a bigger organization, where hundreds or thousands of searches could be conducted every day, otherwise it will be an expensive system to the Indian organizations. It also eliminates the damages, which normally occur by human handling, but also saves a lot of time in loading and unloading the disks.

Publishing Medium

In retrospect, the belief that information technology would lead to the paperless office in the eighties is now slightly embarrassing when we consider that it led to even greater consumption of paper. It is now clear that optical storage techniques will be highly influential in moulding the paperless office. Rewritable optical storage devices lie at the heart of electronic filing systems such as Canon's Canofile, a desktop electronic filing system.

With CD-ROM we are now faced with the equally debatable prospect of a 'paperless' library. CD-ROM is a great deal more than a substitute for paper. Hypertext retrieval systems allow users to exploit textual information more fully. Hypermedia is also possible through CD-ROM.

At a more basic level, greater flexibility than paper is achieved, where information can be accessed randomly and instantly. However, CD-ROM is not without disadvantages. Many users are unable to read from domestic television screens (using CDTV, for instance) for more than an hour or so. Some comfort is gained from the fact that the majority of CD-ROM drives are installed in systems connected to monitors, although, these cannot always be taken as a significant improvement, because they fail to emulate paper sufficiently well.

High specification computer monitors offer one solution, but these are far from widespread at present for reasons of cost. However, the comparatively poor domestic television of today is likely to be superseded by high definition television (HDTV).

The first impact of this will be on multimedia and interactive video systems.

Portability is an important prerequisite for any medium which is to take over from paper. An affordable book-sized CD-ROM reader simply has to materialize. More than just affordable, it has to be reasonably sophisticated and incorporate an appropriately sized display which is both sharp and fast.

9.8.2 CD-ROM standards

Virtually all commercially successful technologies are products of workable standards able to unite manufacturers and yield a user base, sharing a common bond. Two notable examples include videocassette players and audio CD players, both of which have rapidly gained worldwide acceptance.

Often the path to standardization is strewn with obstacles as manufacturers commit themselves to particular technologies or approaches. Sony, for instance, is well known as having once backed the BetaMax VCR only to be squeezed out of the market by VHS players.

Left to industry, resultant standardization need not be the best, but simply the one with most backing in terms of 'software'. It can be argued, for instance, that the immensely successful VHS video standard was quite inferior to competing technologies, and that the IBM PC was a far cry from being the best machine of its time. Besides, what sort of a standard is VHS when UK and US VHS tapes are not interchangeable?

For the developer, it is not necessary to understand the intricate detail of every (emerging) standard, but merely to be made aware of their existence, through which the necessary or largest market for a product can be addressed, which today means ISO 9660. For example, an ISO 9660 title can often be converted between the PC, Macintosh or CDTV, by modifying the retrieval system alone. The cost of converting an ISO disk to CD-I can be considerable.

The announcement of CD-ROM as a storage device in 1983 was accompanied by several fundamental problems, not least of which was a standard physical format and a standard file structure for storing alphanumeric data. There was also the problem of accessing the full data capacity of a CD-ROM through DOS, as existing versions were confined to storage devices with a maximum of 32 Mbytes. The worldwide standard and solution to this latter dilemma is thought of as the MS-DOS CD-ROM Extensions.

Created by Philips and Sony, the Yellow Book is an early standard dealing with the physical format of disks. Later, standard file structures came as a result of industry cooperation in 1985 by way of the High Sierra Group (HSG) standard. This was built upon by ISO to become ISO 9660. For applications devoid of video, and outside the boundaries of multimedia, ISO remains effective. Along with Apple HFS and CD-I, it is accommodated by many replication companies. The latest addition to the CD continuum is the Electronic Book (EB) format.

9.8.3 MS-DOS CD-ROM extensions

An additional device driver and an interface module developed to meet the demands of CD-ROM, are known as the MS-DOS CD-ROM Extensions. The CD-ROM Extensions enable exploitation of the full CD-ROM data capacity, as opposed to 32 Mbyte chunks.

Prior to the CD-ROM Extensions, the situation was rather chaotic, with each drive manufacturer supplying programs that would swap individual 32 Mbyte chunks.

In one sense CD-ROM was actually being used like a number of small mass storage devices, negating its fundamental advantage. Commercial solutions to this problem did emerge, however. One of which came from TMS Inc., by way of LaserDos. This permitted access to the full data capacity, and also supported conventional DOS commands such as DIR.

9.8.4 Technical overview

MS-DOS consists of a number of block device drivers able to support rewritable storage devices such as floppy disk drives and hard disks. These, however, are unsuitable for CD-ROM due to several reasons:

- The full capacity of CD-ROM is not made available;
- MS-DOS utilities become inoperative because files and directories are not in the correct format;
- CD-ROM is not a rewritable medium;
- CD-ROM cannot take advantage of a standard File Allocation Table (FAT), because blocks are addressed differently;
- The method of assignment of drive letters to individual drivers is inappropriate.

MS-DOS, however, can accommodate a character device driver, which reads data as a stream of bytes, and is used to support serial devices such as modems. Unlike block device drivers, these are assigned names as opposed to driver letters. They do not support removable media, and do not accommodate multiple devices.

In essence, an effective CD-ROM device driver is a character device driver which has been modified to accommodate drive letters, an eight-byte character device name, and number of devices or units supposed. The standard MS-DOS character device driver command set is enhanced to include commands specific to CD-ROM (See Table).

Table

Device Driver Commands Codes

Command Code	Name
0	INIT
3	IOCTL INPUT
7	INPUT FLUSH
12	IOCTL OUTPUT
13	DEVICE OPEN
14	DEVICE CLOSE
128	READ LOG
129	RESERVED
130	READ LONG PREFETCH
131	SEEK
132	PLAY
133	STOP PLAY

The installation of a CD-ROM driver requires an appropriate device entry in the CONFIG.SYS file which typically approximates to the following:

DEVICE=C:/DEC/NEC.SYS/D:MSCD000/N:1

Such a statement causes DOS to lead the device driver NEC.SYS included in the DRIVE directory.

Designing a multi-user system or networking of CD-ROMs is not possible for any library or organization, because their main objective is to provide information rather than designing the systems. It is also very difficult to find out a system which meets complete needs of any organization, but which meets maximum needs of the people, with a reasonable cost. Before choosing a suitable CD-ROM system for an organization, one should look into the following factors: (i) single or multi-user system, (ii) maintenance support, (iii) obsolescent equipment, (iv) reliability, (v) user satisfaction, and (vi) warranty period.[9]

Since the amount of investment is fairly large on this equipment, considerable support in terms of continuing advice, as well as dependable maintenance should be required.

81 CD-ROM *Vs* Online Searching

CD-ROM	Online Searching
(i) Menu-driven, user friendly, slow software.	Command driven.
(ii) Diagrams, charts, maps, illustrations, etc. possible.	Graphs, charts, maps, illustrations, etc. are not possible, textual information only (for the time being).
(iii) One time cost.	Cost proportional to usage of the databases.
(iv) Updation takes time and costs lot of money.	Frequent updation of databases.

9.9 Indian Networks

India's first data communications and computer network (INDONET) was commissioned in 1986 by CMC Ltd. In the first phase, mainly they have networked Bombay, Calcutta and

Madras; after some time New Delhi and Hyderabad was also linked as additional stations. INDONET is presently having an International Gateway which is providing access to worldwide packet switched networks like USA's Global Network Systems (GNS), TELNET and INTERNET, Singapore's TELEPAC and Germany's DATEX-P (ROY, A. 1989). With the present network one can access the information from the world's major databases such as NTIS, INSPEC, ERIC, COMPENDEX, MEDLINE and CLAMS. It is a costly affair. CD-ROM Lan System has solved this problem. Once the system is installed and connected to a network, such as INDONET or ERNET, any user of this network will access the information easily and save a lot of budget. Several organizations have joined networks such as BTISNET, CALIBNET, SIRNET, DESINET, ERNET, INFLIBNET, VIDYANNET, etc. It is better to develop the CD-ROM collections in their own fields first, afterwards install a CD-ROM LAN system, so that all the users of these networks will access other's database.

NOTES

1. Scott A. Gield. "Multiuser CD-ROM system for libraries". Laswer disc professional. 2, 1989; pp. 14-17.
2. Gord Nickerson. "Remote access to CD-ROM." *CD-ROM End User*. 1,1989; pp. 23-46.
3. John M. Herney. "A comparison of different CD-ROM Local Area Networks in Universities". *CD-ROM End User*. 1, 1989; pp. 17-22.
4. C.K. Ramaiah. "Adoption of CD-ROM in libraries." *DESIDOC Bulletin*. 9, 1989; pp. 3-11.
5. A. Ray. "Computer networking in developing countries." CMC's INDONET. International Online Meeting 13th, London, Dec. 12-14, 1989. *Oxford Learners Information*, 1989; pp. 567-585.
6. John M. Harney. "A comparison of different CD-ROM Local Area Network in Universities." *CD-ROM End User*. 1, 1989; pp. 17-22.
7. C.K. Ramaiah. "Adoption of CD-ROM in libraries." *DESIDOC Bulletin* 9, 1989; pp. 3-10.
8. M.A. Grant. "Multi-Platter CD-ROM at Boston College". *Laserdisc Professional*. 2, 1989; pp. 12-16.
9. A. Ray. "Computer networking in developing countries." CMC INDONET. 13th Inter Conference London. Dec. 12, 1989; p. 4. *Oxford Learners Information*; pp. 563-75.

Bibliometrics

10

10.1 Introduction

In 1969 Pritchard coined a new term—'bibliometrics'—for a type of study that had been in existence for half a century. A new field of quantitative analysis had emerged; it has applied mathematical and statistical methods to books and other means of printed communication. Bibliometrics has become the generic term for a whole range of specific measurements and indicators. Its purpose is to measure the output of scientific and technological research through data derived not only from scientific literature but from patents as well. Bibliometric approaches are based on the notion that the essence of scientific research is the communication of new contributions to the body of knowledge in scientific literature. Patents indicate a transfer of knowledge to industrial innovation and a transformation into something of economic and social value. According to Price, a scientist is "...any person who has published a scientific paper".[1]

In 1970s there was a quantum leap in the number of bibliometric studies initiated by the coming into existence of a database of scientific publications, the Science Citation Index (SCI). Its initial idea was to give researchers a quick and effective way to find published articles in their field of research.[2] It has three advantages:

(1) SCI covers all science fields. SCI coverage is unambiguous because every item from every journal is indexed.

(2) All author addresses listed on the paper are included in the SCI. This is a necessity for studying institutional output, as collaboration is so extensive.

(3) References are included in the SCI and only the SCI. Citation counts can be derived from these references and used as a partial indicator of the impact previous research has had on succeeding work.

A second important step in the development of scientometrics came in the 1980s with the introduction of co-word analysis. Co-word analysis was developed by proponents of social constructivism and the technique is as theory-laden as any scientific tool.[3] (1) that technology is heterogeneous, that there is no way to separate the scientific from the social and political. The scientist is an interest-driven person who uses whatever resources are available, from social influence to raw data, to reach some profit, (2) that technology is an emergent phenomena without any autonomously set trajectory. Rather, it is shaped by a web of social and technical forces every set up of the way, (3) that the primary tool of scientists, the weapon used to exert force on the socio-technical web, is the text. A successful scientific paper is one which links entities in new ways and exerts enough force to convince other scientists to believe in this linkage. We can think of a scientific paper as a network of important words.

Co-citation analysis has traditionally been linked with the ISI Science Citation Index and has mainly been concerned with the evaluation of scientific activities. Co-citation occurs when two publications are cited by a third, later publication. The greater the frequency of co-citation of a given pair, the greater the likelihood that it defines an established or emerging topic or subspeciality. The citation pair can be used in a citation index search to retrieve related publications. One pair can usually identify a small research front, but active research fronts generally involve several interrelated co-citation pairs. The larger the number of pairs included in a cluster, the broader the scope.

Bibliometrics, so successful at portraying research output and impact, can be used to develop new indicators with great potential to address emerging concerns such as institutional level analysis of capabilities and networks. As with any type of data, bibliometric indicators will not provide a perfect, ideal picture of the processes. However, they can make a unique contribution to pictures compiled from multiple sources, providing an unrivalled objective, disaggregated and internationally comparable time series signature of networks and capabilities. Classical bibliometrics focuses on the national level and international comparisons. Even with the emerging emphasis on disaggregation, international comparison and analysis of interdependencies will be required. The sectoral and intra-sectoral level data developed are possible due to recent advances in desktop computing. These data can make their most powerful contribution in the context of the new approaches to innovation.

A glimpse of the value of bibliometric indicators may be provided for exploring science, technology and innovation systems.

Polanco (personal communication) suggested the following scheme to summarize the various dimensions of scientometric methodologies.

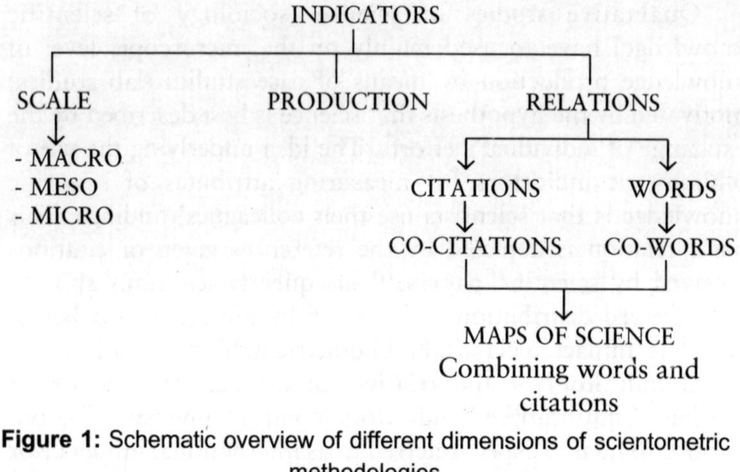

Figure 1: Schematic overview of different dimensions of scientometric methodologies

Bibliometrics is a tool by which the state of science and technology can be observed through the traces of communication in the science-technology system, most notably the published papers in referred journals. Originally, it was meant for the situation of a country in relation to the world, and institution in relation to a country. The focus of quantitative analysis of a country in relation to the world, and institution in relation to country. The focus of quantitative analysis of scientific development shifted more and more to the mapping of scientific development in interaction with social, political and economic developments; the so-called second generation indicators. These scientometric indicators are equally suitable for 'macro' analysis and 'micro' studies.

Knowledge is produced by recombinations and associations of existing papers. New knowledge claims are related to previous research by means of cited references. It follows that there are some advantages to looking at science in its textual form. Printed papers not only provide a wide accessibility and dissemination of knowledge, it has also more fundamental attributes that legitimate it to be the focus of analysis. It provides a more codified mode of communication than other media. This raises some interesting issues for the quantitative analysis of electronic communications.

Qualitative studies of science (sociology of scientific knowledge) have focused mainly on the microscopic level of knowledge production by means of case studies (lab studies) motivated by the hypothesis that science is best described by the exchange of individual's efforts. The idea underlying the use of bibliometric indicators for measuring attributes of scientific knowledge is that scientists use their colleagues' findings. This basic relation is depicted by the references given or citations received by scientific papers. Consequently, citations show a very skewed distribution as is shown by impact or number of citations. Impact, a classical bibliometric indicator, is a citation-based indicator for the relative importance of a paper or journal. Citation-based indicators point to one specific, but important quality aspect referred to as international influence or impact.

The enterprise of science is best captured by the concept of an evolving communication system. Processes of feedback and of self-reference are vital in maintaining a special system. Scientific communications can be represented by two information cycles. The first-primary-cycle is the process of submission to journals and peer review. Scientific communication can also be communicated reflexively, by measuring scientometric attributes of the communications, which in turn can be communicated. In terms of the information cycle representation, the indicators appear in the form of second cycle. This cycle processes information about the primary information cycle, in the form of meta-information.

Bibliometric analysis beyond publication counts, tools to conduct co-citation and co-word analysis developed and applied to cross national comparisons. These methods provide data that allow analysis to 'map' centers of scientific excellence and to show trends and developments in scientific thought. Co-citation analysis involves identifying pairs or groups of articles that are cited together in other articles or publications as cited in the Science Citation Index. This analysis allows for examination of many facets of national scientific activity, including scientific collaboration, the relative strength of centers of research as viewed by peers, and the importance of a scientific contribution over time.

Co-word analysis involves assigning keywords to a paper or article and conducting frequency analysis on the words chosen. These methods identify 'emerging' words—those which indicate recent developments—by using conference papers instead of a journal set or publications. Despite its promise as a more precise indicator than citation counts, the use of co-word analysis is controversial among scholars. Words and classifications are an order of magnitude less specific than citations as a static indicator of the output of science. There are two examples of indicators 'Jacaard Index' and 'inclusion index'.

The clusters of dense communications can be identified as disciplines and within those disciplines specialities. The concept of membership of scientific communication has been a major theme in science studies. In sociology of science, the endeavor has been abandoned altogether, arguing that boundaries take shape in local and temporary situations.

A method for empirical analysis of evolving scientific communication systems has been developed that reflects the phenomena of systems boundaries and identity construction. Using aggregated journal-journal citations, the citational environment of the entrance journal can be defined as all journals that cite or are cited by this journal above a threshold percentage. Factor analysis reveals clearly identifiable clusters of journals representing scientific disciplines. Groups of scientific journals define certain scientific disciplines or paradigms. The use of references and title words within this group of journals is highly codified, which results in skewed distribution of cited references, title-words, publications per journal, publications per author, publications per country, etc. These scientific specialists are expected to behave as self-organizing communication systems that maintain some kind of 'plastic identity'. The characteristics of a cluster of journals, 'a scientific speciality', and its development in relation to its journal environment can provide quantitative indicators for the degree of interdisciplinarity.

10.2 Research Topics

Scientometric indicators like cited references and (title) words can be distinguished by the way they refer to different levels of the textual organization. From an evolutionary perspective on scientific communication, the text—that is words and co-words—provide the variation. References and citations can therefore be considered indicators of these selection processes. The way researchers draw on earlier works, and their sharing of a set of exemplars, is considered to be reflected in the referencing practices of the speciality members.

Where the larger research fields can be operationalized as journals systems, research topics are a much lower level of aggregation, of (new) knowledge claims with respect to the topic under study. Research topics can be defined as document systems using a relevant criterion, it enables us to investigate the cognitive dimension of the system with institutional dimensions of the system to investigate network formation within the STI system, based on the interaction of institutional factors and cognitive factors.

Bibliometric maps of Science are landscapes of scientific research fields created by quantitative analysis of bibliometric data. In such maps the 'cities' are, for instance, research topics. Data derived from co-citation and co-word analysis enable analysts to perform multidimensional scaling (MDS) and mapping of scientific activity.

Databases do not carry all published materials, for example. What is carried may not have complete citations. All-author citations can lead to double counting, and obligatory citations to colleagues or professors can distort the counts. Co-word citation analysis depends upon subjective choice of key words and so is subject to bias. Scholars are working on techniques to remove distortions from these indicators. Even so, bibliometric indicators are, by definition, "statistical proxies for unmeasured parameters in a complex economic, political and social system of knowledge production.

10.3 Research Collaboration

Paper counts provide a very simplified and approximate measure of the quantity of scientific output. It has been noted that the number of scientific publications has been growing exponentially since their coming into existence. The output in the number of papers per region or country provides a crude measure of the geographical distribution of knowledge production. The number of co-authors on a paper is a measure of co-operation at a national or international level. International co-authorship, in general, results in publications with higher citation rates than purely domestic papers. International collaboration has, however, not the same influence on publication profiles and citation impact of each analyzed country.

10.4 Change in Knowledge Production

According to OECD report ICT related changes underlying the evolving science system have three main sources; technological change in the ICT industry; scientists' efforts to develop their own tools; and government programs specifically designed to foster developments in ICT and apply them to scientific needs. The main technological developments that make this evolution possible are identified; cheaper processing capacity and more user-friendly software tools, increased storage capacity and information delivery technologies, and finally electronic networks that constitute the infrastructure which provides scientists with new means of communication.

More important factories have adopted the shift in communication technologies from print to computer. Great changes in human consciousness have always accompanied changes in forms of communication human beings use to create their social relations. The last great shift in communication technologies, from oral to print culture, came at the dawn of the modern era and changed forever the nature of human consciousness. The print revolution facilitated a way of thinking that was ideally suited to a society of reason and progress.[4] The mnemonic redundancy of oral communication and the subjective eccentricities of medieval script were replaced by a more rational, calculating, analytical approach to knowledge. Print replaced human memory with tables of contents, pagination, footnotes, and indexes. Print organizes phenomena in an orderly, rational, and objective way, and in so doing encourages linear, sequential, and casual way of thinking. In sum, print culture introduces knowledge that can be communicated, reproduced and recombined independent from individuals: the birth of science.

Electronic communication is organized cybernetically, not linearly. The notion of sequentiality and casuality are replaced by a total field of continuous, integrated activity. In an electronic world of communications, subjects and objects give way to nodes and networks, and structure and functions are subsumed processes. Hypertext replaces the more limited and narrow kind of print referencing. A printed book is exclusive in nature and autonomous in form. Hypertext, however, is inclusive in nature and relational in form. Hypertext is merely a starting point from which users make connections between related materials. It is never complete. The printed book is a product, while hypertext is a process.

Researchers are developing new information and communication pattern. This revolution finds its roots in the intimate interaction between information and communication technologies (ICT), and advanced scientific and technological research and innovation. Information is a resource, raw material and output in the process of knowledge production. This informational turn in the sciences coincides with the processes of commercialization and commodification of scientific knowledge, the new hybrid roles of academic research institutes and universities, a wider variety of types of research output and more attention to norms and values.

Consequently, the processes and operations that maintain the science system are changing. The validation boundaries emerging from the differences between classical and new modes of knowledge production are changing. The new mode of knowledge production is more heterogeneous in nature; quality control is no longer simply a matter of peer review; consensus is formed outside traditional disciplinary boundaries; and research outcomes are influenced by social accountability. Due to the nature of the print medium, scientific papers are very well codified. It is easy to identify whether or not a paper is communicated within the science system, whether it is scientific or not. Although the reasons that cited references are used can be very diverse on the level of individual scientists, it provides a very clear, unambiguous representation of the shared knowledge base of a scientific discipline.

The linking patterns of universities and research institutes might provide immediate information about the context or knowledge production. The knowledge networks that can be mapped on the web do not have any equivalent in print media. Citations do not provide us with an accurate representation of technological achievements, because knowledge can be built into technological artifacts without necessarily leaving the formal trace of a citation in the scientific literature. It becomes clear that new methodologies, concepts and theories are required to deal with changing nature of scientific knowledge production and communication. On one hand, scientific research provides new tools, database, equipment and media that in turn influence the production of knowledge. The concept of science as an evolving communication system that has been introduced above can be useful in understanding these developments.

10.5 From Bibliometrics to Webometrics

Bibliometrics are still widely used as a generic term for the corrected fields of sciento-, info-, techno- metrics where publications are considered the elementary units of scientific information and the main source of indicators.

E-journals

Electronic journals provide an excellent opportunity for quantitative analysis similar to the bibliometric analysis of print articles. Most electronic journals are internet versions of existing print journals. The print based scientometric indicators could be applied to these journals. There are some communicational aspects of e-journals that could modify the emerging patterns; as electronic publications permit more flexibility and speed in the dissemination of scientific information. E-journals provide new kind of analysis. How often are papers changed and updated after initial submission? How extensive are the changes? What proportion of preprints are replaced by peer reviewed reprints?

Intermediate Communications

Publishing the results of scientific research was a symbiotic interaction between researchers and publishers, because the most effective way scientists could disseminate their results was through journals, produced by professional societies and independent publishers. Electronic communication has created new ways to distribute such results and is forcing researchers and publishers to reassess the old procedures and consider new possibilities as we learn to use the Internet.

Internet

The third option for bibliometric analysis of the science, technology and innovation system on the internet is using websites in general, not necessarily e-journals. This immediately poses the problem of the unit of analysis. In print communications, papers are communicated in journals.

A website comprising hierarchically grouped pages, and represented by the URL address of the highest level, is considered as a unit. It is identified as formally different from other websites and is recognizable as representing a research group with the aim of being present at the web. The institutional character of the proposed new unit eases comparative analysis with external data, as usually there are scientometric analyses available following that institutional grouping criterion.

However, one of the main problems of webometrics in this context is related to the 'codification of knowledge'. Common languages allow for one layer of reflexivity without confusion. Codification in specialist, scientific languages allows for the stabilization of meaning in nearly decomposable reflexive layers of communication. In other words, scientific communications are more codified than non-scientific communications. The meaning of 'words' and 'cited references' are less ambiguous and scientific context words and references remain ambiguous in their meaning. The web is an information space quite different from common scientific and professional databases, the similarities between electronic and print media are often superficial. Most notably, time plays a different role on the web.

There are two layers of communication system:

(1) Most probably a "two-tier system" will evolve. The first tier is a "free space" for preprints and other "preliminary" communications. It is a representation of the scientific enterprise in "real time". The second tier is the world of more formal publications. The first tier is the place where informal and formal communications will become closely connected.[5]

(2) The 'second tier' of scientific communication will consist largely of already existing journals, of which most soon we will have a print as well as an electronic form.

10.6 Electronic Indicators

Bibliometric indicators are used in studying the development of the science system.

10.6.1 Collective production of scientific knowledge

They look into citation analysis, i.e., link page analysis in terms of Rousseau (1997) and web impact factor studies. The world-wide-web may revolutionize the way scientists communicate with each other. More and more researchers publish original work on the www rather than publication in paper journals. It is difficult to evaluate the quality of the published paper—as opposed to traditional publishing, where for example the scientific "rank" of the journal is known. In traditional (paper) publishing, scientometric indicators such as the impact factor are based on bibliometric analysis and serve as quality indicators for published scientific work. The SCI does not take into account electronic works published on the www. Attempts have been made to develop a WCI (Web Citation Index). It is important to understand that the Web Citation Index does strictly focus on scholarly works published on the web and does not include "generic" webpages or whole websites.

Candidates for indicators could be remote files retrieval counts or clients hypertext links counts. These can point to "classical" links like citations or author's addresses but they can also assume new forms like the "annotation" or the "is-interested-in" links available on www. Similar indicators can be devised in order to assess the impact of information servers or services offered.

10.6.2 Coordination mechanisms

The levels, direction, number, relations, use and the life span of links between sites are all indicators for the nature of clustering of websites. The meaning and significance of citation is expected to be quite different in the two environments of scholarly publishing and the www. The question is whether the types of intellectual mapping of disciplines made possible with citation indexes like Science Citation Index (SCI) and co-citation techniques might be applied to charting the contents of cyberspace. Counts of ingoing and outgoing links can be seen as citation and reference analysis respectively.[6] However, due to its dynamic and distributed nature, the web often demonstrates web pages simultaneously linking to each other—a case not possible in the traditional paper-based citation world. Ingwersen[7] introduces the application of informetric methods to the world wide web (www) also called intermetrometrics.

10.6.3 Disciplines and specialities

There are three main directions to perform knowledge discovery on the web, a set of methodologies to find related clusters of communications. They are concerned with exploiting (1) webage content, (2) link structures, and (3) users' information behaviour (searching and browsing). Their focus is mainly on the exploitation of link structures—an approach with strong kinship to bibliometric citation analysis, but not only by means of strong ties. They point out that links weave together web documents in a complex structured hypertext corpus. Link structures represent implicit human 'annotations' that can be exploited for knowledge discovery, for example inferring web communities,[8] identifying authorative web pages or improving search engine ranking algorithms.

10.6.4 Research topics

Words and co-words can serve as a basis for bibliometric analysis on the web just as in the print world. Again, the (lack of) codification of electronic communication poses a challenge to quantitative analysis. However, besides the words, web pages contain other information in the source code, like key words, that might provide additional and more codified sources of information for analysis.

Geographical distribution

The geographical location of a site, publication or person on the web is hard to determine unambiguously since we will not be counting corporate sources but "electronic addresses". There is no assurance that they represent only one person or indeed always the same person. Some information services offer only "hosts access count" and, a host may serve up to hundreds of users. The URLs of websites often do provide information about the location and or the type of institution.

For Example: www.*com (Industrial text)
www.*ed (Education text)
www.*gov (Government texts)

10.6.5 E-Journals and webometrics

Due to the increasing amount of information available free or nearly free on the web, scientists are concerned with the application of bibliometrics on the web. Webometrics displays several similarities to informetric and scientometric studies and the application of common bibliometric methods. The content analysis of web pages corresponds to traditional publication analysis. Counts and analysis of outgoing links from web pages (outlinks) and of links pointing to web pages (inlinks) can be seen as reference and citation analysis. Outlinks and inlinks are then similar to references and citations, respectively, in scientific articles. Since the web consists of contributions from anyone who wishes to contribute and usual kind of peer reviewing is missing, the quality of information or the knowledge value often cannot be determined or is problematic. But citation, like link analysis, may reveal clusters of sites to be reviewed. Webometrics can be performed for identification of relevant articles or electronic journals, for mapping a field of interest as well as for determination of the impact of scientific work on research. One part of webometrics focuses on electronic journals as the counterpart of printed journals. Aim of these investigations is to determine the importance of e-journals for scientific research compared with print media based on citation analysis.

E-Journals

Besides demographic parameters like the number of articles published, the number of subscriptions, the discipline, the number of articles downloaded or the charging policy, the main indicator used is the impact factor based on citation analysis.

ISI (Institute of Scientific Information) publishes three citation indexes: Science Citation Index SCI, Social Science Citation Index (SSCI) and Arts and Humanities Citation Index (AHCI). Only a few electronic journals are covered by ISI. Furthermore, using ISI for evaluation of the impact factor of electronic publications one has to take into account that only references in (important) journals are counted as citations. Hyperlinks to web pages are not included. If we compare the impact of citations of scientific articles published in e-journals and print media,[9] it includes:

(a) Citation analysis calculator

(b) Impact factor

(c) Immediacy factor

(d) Total number of articles

The impact factor measures the current impact of the typical recently published articles in a particular journal. For example, the impact factor of a journal in 1995 can be calculated using the following equation:

Example:

Impact factor for 1995 =

$$\frac{\text{(No. of citations received in 1995 to 1993 \& 1994 articles)}}{\text{(Number of articles published in 1993 and 1994)}}$$

Immediacy index for 1995 =

$$\frac{\text{(Number of citations received in 1995 to 1995 articles)}}{\text{(Number of 1995 onwards)}}$$

Determining the different indicators is based on the following steps:

- Selection of several e-journals.
- Identification of relevant titles in science, technology, and medicine (STM) fields.
- Search for the number of citations to the selected titles in the JCR and ISI's Web of Science database.
- Determination of the different indicators.

Example: Eight out of 39 e-journals which were cited ten or more times over their lifetime (Table 1).

Table 1

The eight most highly cited e-journals[10]

Name of e-journal	Discipline	Print Version	No. of citations to the e-journals
Bulletin of the American Mathematical Society	Mathematics	Yes	>1,500
Online Journal of Current Clinical Trials	Medicine	No	190
The Public Access Computer System Review	Library and Information Sc.	Yes	111
Digital Technical Journal	Computer Science	No	38
Psycology	Psychology	No	35
Interpersonal Computing and Technology	Effects of technology on society	No	14
Electronic Journal of Communication	Communication	No	11
Postmodern Culture	Modern Culture	No	10

Above table determines a very low impact of e-journals on scholarly communication compared with printed articles. Table 2 shows the results for the impact factor, the immediacy factor and the number of current articles of medical journals in the ISI's Citation Reports 1998.

Table 2

Comparisons of the 1999 Impact Factor, Immediacy Index, and Number of Current Articles of Medical Free Scholarly Electronic Journals with the 99th, 90th, 75th, 50th, and 25th percentile Medical journals in ISI's journal Citation Reports 1998. For the British Medical Journal, 1998 JCR data is reported for that title instead of 1999 data.[11]

	Impact Factor		Immediacy Index		Current Articles
99th	**42.93**	**99th**	**7.28**	**99th**	**1681**
Emerging Infectious Diseases	7.17	British Medical Journal	2.03	British Medical Journal	916
British Medical Journal	5.33	Emerging Infectious Diseases	0.95	Southern Medical Journal	312
Blood, Cells, Molecules Diseases	4.77	Medicine and Global Survival	0.60	**90th**	**261**
Alzheimer's Disease Review	4.38	**90th**	**0.49**	Radiographics	196
90th	**3.03**	**75th**	**0.27**	**75th**	**149**
Radiographics	1.88	Radiographics	0.16	Emerging Infectious Diseases	123
75th	**1.81**	Blood, Cells, Molecules Diseases	0.14	Annals of Saudi Medicine	122
Eurosurveillance	1.71	Eurosurveillance	0.14	**50th**	73
Southern Medical Journal	1.01	**50th**	**0.12**	Blood, Cells, Molecules Diseases	42
50th	0.94	**25th**	**0.04**	**25th**	38
25th	**0.44**	Southern Medical Journal	0.02	Eurosurveillance	37
Annals of Saudi Medicine	0.24	Annals of Saudi Medicine	0.01	Online Journal of Issues in Nursing	29
Dermatology Online	0.06	Alzheimer's Disease Review	0	Dermatology Online	8
Online Journals of Issues in Nursing	0.03	Dermatology Online	0	Alzheimer's Disease Review	6
Medicine and Global Survival	0	Online Journal of Issues in Nursing	0	Medicine and Global Survival	5

Web Publications

There are three main directions to perform knowledge discovery on the web:

(a) Web page contents,
(b) Link structures, and
(c) User's information behaviour (i.e., searching and browsing).

The exploitation of link structure is closely tied to bibliometric citation analysis.

A description of the linking pattern, based on the web topology, is given below:

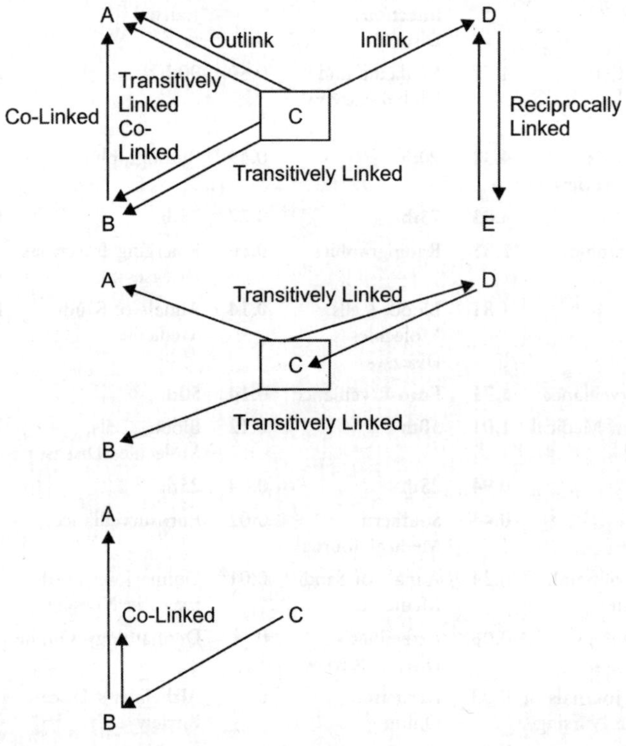

Linking Pattern

Based on the graph above the link pattern is:

- C has an outlink to A.
- C has an inlink from D.
- D and E are reciprocally linked.
- D is transitively linked with A and B through C.
- A and B are co-linked from C (co-citation).
- B and C are co-linking to A (bibliographic coupling).

The co-citation analysis is based on the assumption that if two references are cited together, in a latter literature, the two references are themselves related. The major refinement between bibliometric coupling and co-citation is that while coupling measures the relationship between source documents, co-citation measures the relations between cited documents. Using those definitions the co-link searches can be performed by:

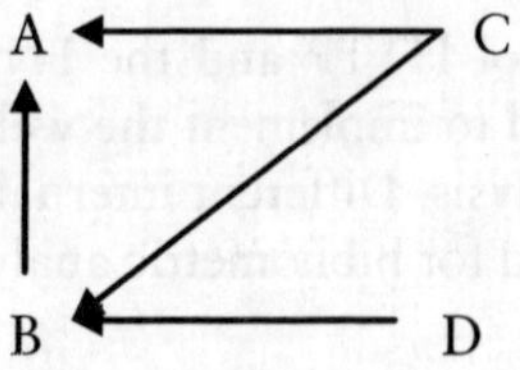

Co-citation
- AB linked with C
- B co-linked with C and D

For investigating the link structures on the web graph, theoretic methods can be used. The topology of link structures affects possibilities for human and digital agents to traverse and explore the Web. Link topology as:

- levels: different web analysis entities: web pages, hosts, domains
- direction: inlinks/outlinks––unidirectional/reciprocal
- number: one, two, many inlinks or outlinks
- relations: analogy with citations; reflect social attitudes and interest; linkage motives
- use: strong and weak links: more or less used: “the learning web”.

In graph theory, a graph is a mathematical representation of a network consisting of vertices (or nodes) connected by edges. The nodes can be Internet servers, documents (in a citation network), concepts (in a thesaurus or semantic network), etc. In a directed graph the edges represent directional relations between the nodes. The Web is an example of a directed graph with web pages corresponding to nodes and hyperlinks to edges. Graph theoretic methods can be used to analyse structural aspects of the web.

One of the first scientists dealing with webometrics and graph theory was Abraham (1997). Abraham's strategy for visualizing and measuring the web is based on the mathematics of morphogenesis, complex dynamical systems theory. The strategy is based on the fact that the web can be described as a tree consisting of domains, servers, and pages. There are tens of thousands of domains, several servers in each domain, and many pages in each server. Each domain has a unique name and each page has a unique URL. These are the main choices for nodes of the web.

The Hyper Text Transfer Protocol HTTP and the Hyper Text Markup Language HTML—used to implement the web—were used to perform informetric analysis. Different internal or external server information can be used for bibliometric analysis such as:[12]

- email logs to and from the system administrator (the data size and times, not necessarily the content);
- program usage logs;
- server-based—the log file created by the web server itself;
- proxy-based—via a firewall (additional layer of server protection) or some server controlled access systems;
- client-based—via client application code that can record and transmit information to the server such as cookies;
- network-based—the programs that control system-level networking security and access on the server.

While in the ISI's citation databases descriptors are found in the three forms: Author Keyword, Key Words Plus and Research Fronts, on the web descriptors are given either by an author or by frequencies. For the subject access points of the web pages an author can use tags, such as <em> and <strong>. Frequencies of terms are measured by some web indexes. The titles of the web pages are found either within the <TITLE> or/and <H1> tag, and can uniquely be identified by the URL of the page. Whether the author is a person or corporate source can only be identified manually. Corporate source or affiliation for web pages is given by the first part of the URL, but the institution hosting a web page is not necessarily connected with the author of the web page.

Web Impact Factor studies use of hypertext links, which are measured by search engines such as AltaVista, rather than bibliographic citations. Web Impact Factors have been shown to be useful measures of the influence of sites belonging to organizations such as universities and research institutes.

Webometric studies have used large-scale web search engines such as AltaVista. These allow measurements to be made of the total number of pages in a domain or a set of directories, such as the pages in the directories and subdirectories and the links between them. Web search engines provide similar possibilities for the investigation of links between documents to those provided by the citation databases created by the Institute for Scientific Information.

A 'Web Impact Factor' is the number of pages linking to a web space, divided by the number of pages in the web space. The WIF differs in respect to the time period from the journal Impact Factor, which is constrained by the methods used to compile citation indexes. The journal impact factor measures citations made in journals published during one time period, to articles published in another time period. The WIF, in contrast, is a "snapshot" from the search engine database of all links to a web space at the time of measurement.

The web pages are analysed corresponding to their links internally and/or externally and the numbers of links is obtained. This method is up to now used from most of the bibliometric researchers. The problems which have arisen using this method are besides others:

- inconsistency of different combinations of search operators;
- dependence of the amount of identified web pages on the time of the search;
- duplicates of web pages and self citation;
- dependence of the search results on the search engine applied for the citation analysis.

10.6.6 Webometric studies

In several fields like health and medical domains "quality control" is of great concern due to the fact that the web allows great freedom in information dissemination and linking and lacks any peer-reviewing. Everyone can link to web pages he wants to. This on the one hand allows countries and regions with otherwise low infrastructure to contribute in (scientific) communication, on the other hand great uncertainty is created to the users. (Bjorneborn and Ingwersen, 2000). Therefore, the importance of methods and indicators which allow an evaluation of the information found on the web, increases.

Analysis of university-industry-government relations

Search commands used for analysis of sub-domain web servers

Keyword	Function
host: name	Finds pages on a specific computer. The search host: altavista.digital.com would find pages on the AltaVista computer, and host: dilbert.unitedmedia.com would find pages on the computer called dilbert at unitedmedia.com.
Link: URLtext	Finds pages with a link to a page with the specified URL text. Use link: altavista.digital.com to find all pages linking to AltaVista.
Text:text	Finds pages that contain the specified text in any part of the page other than an image tag, link, or URL. The search text:cow9 would find all pages with the term cow9 in them.

The following indicators for analysis of the relationship between industry, university and government in the Netherlands and Brazil using the Alta Vista Advanced Search Engine:

- Amount of websites.
- Consideration of the languages used.
- Searching for specific hyperlinks between .com, .edu and .gov sites.
- Analysis of time dependence (1993-1998).
- Analysis of the links between pages (Alta Vista search link….).
- Search for words / co-words using the full text respectively the titles.

Four search functions of Alta Vista were used: domain, link, text and title.

Medical Websites

Cui (1999)[13] performed a bibliometric analysis of health care related websites. The analysis focused on the pages linked to in the "other links" section of the web pages of 19 of the top 25 US medical schools. The identified web pages were ranked according to their cited frequency by examining the links made from these pages. The determined links were analysed by a special software program called Checkweb and cleaned up in order to obtain only the active links to external URLs. The frequency of the URLs was counted taking into account the different URL levels.

The results were the distribution of the top-level domains (TLDs), the first level domains and the whole domain name websites. The most highly cited web TLDs are .edu, .com, .gov and .org—all registered in the USA (Table 3). Other countries whose TLDs are frequently cited are UK (.uk), Switzerland (.ch), Canada (.ca), Germany (.de), Australia (.au), Sweden (.se) and Netherlands (.nl). Cui applied the citation analysis and determined the 78 most highly cited websites out of thousands of cited links. He concludes that the method supports librarians and information scientists in evaluating websites.

Table 3

The URLs and the frequency distribution of the "First Level Domains" (Cui, 1999)

Rank	URLs	Frequency	Percent	Cum Percent
1	http://www.yahoo.com	91	2.47	2.47
2	http://www.gen.emory.edu	86	2.33	4.80
3	http://www.cdc.gov	65	1.76	6.56

The authors conclude that some website characteristics as the number of daily visits, their updating frequency and, overall, the number of websites linked to them, correlate with their evaluation by some of the largest rating systems on the Internet, which means that certain indexes obtained from the usage analysis of pediatric websites could be used as quality indicators. On the other hand, the citation analysis on the web by the quantification of inbound links to medical websites could be an objective and feasible tool in rating great amounts of websites.

10.7 Maps

Larson (1996)[14] applied the co-citation analysis for mapping websites based on their hypertext links. The search was performed for websites on the topics geographic information systems, earth sciences, and satellite remote sensing. The steps of analysis were:

1. Selection of the core set of items for the study.
2. Retrieval of co-citation frequency information for the core set.
3. Compilation of the raw co-citation frequency matrix.
4. Correlation analysis to convert the raw frequencies into correlation coefficients.
5. Multivariant analysis of the correlation matrix, using principle components analysis, cluster analysis or multidimensional scaling techniques.

The search was performed with the Alta Vista search engine. The sample he obtained contained 125 websites. He calculated the co-citation matrix, determined the co-occurencies and used multidimensional scaling for mapping of the results.

The mappings produced by co-citation analysis of websites in geographic information systems, earth sciences, and satellite remote-sensing seem to produce quite clear, reasonable and interpretable results.

The discussions about the application of bibliometric of the web point out that several aspects have to be considered calculating the web impact factor WIF or others:

1. While traditionally bibliometric analysis is based on articles published in journals the web does not mainly consist of articles but of web pages with different intention and scientific background.
2. Some studies focused on e-journals and scholarly communication in order to obtain the impact of electronic publications on research in comparison to printed ones. The results have shown that the importance of e-journals for knowledge production has in some research fields increased significantly in the last few years.
3. Bibliometric analysis is mainly performed using search engines for determination of numbers of hosts, links from one domain or web page to others, domains or text corresponding to a specific topic. The search engine used in most cases is Alta Vista because it allows Boolean searches for host, links, domains and combinations of them.
4. The studies have shown that the search results using search engines have to be handled with great care because the numbers obtained depend on the search string. Using several combinations of the same Boolean operators do not provide the same results. This fact has to be considered for bibliometric web analysis. Inconsistencies have been determined depending on the time of the search and the combination of operators or due to search engine results in duplicates.
5. Indicators determined for webometrics are up to now mainly the impact factor and the immediacy factor.

Furthermore, the following information can be determined:

(a) Amount of websites.

(b) Consideration of the languages used.

(c) Searching for specific hyperlinks between .com, .edu and .gov sites (the generic Top Level Domains gTLDs).

(d) Analysis of time dependence.

(e) Analysis of the links between pages.

(f) Search for words/co-words using the full text respectively the titles.

(g) Bibliographic coupling: measuring the number of references two papers have in common to test for similarity.

(h) Cocitation analysis: if two references are cited together, in a latter literature, the two references are themselves related.

6. An additional fundamental difference between print and web based bibliometric analysis is the possibility of an almost continuous change of contents on the web.

10.8 Conclusion

The most complicating factor in webometric research is that of data collection. Data collection on the web depends on the retrieval features of the various search engines and web robots. The commercial search engine cover of the web space by introducing the concept of 'indexable web'. The concept signifies the portion of the web that can be indexed by the engines. The engines do not cover the entire web, the overlap between them is not substantial and their retrieval functions too simplistic for webometric analysis. There is a problem of lack of data. But besides the above-mentioned problem of information retrieval on the web, there are also problems related to methodology and theory. All this activity is taking place inside electronic networks and computers produce them automatically. Most sociological methods of gathering information suppose the laboratory as a site. It is likely that only sites present a suitable unit of analysis in terms of link structures. Universities and other large institutions are likely to have a very heterogeneous and un-codified linking pattern. On the other hand, individuals and small groups will have a unrepresentative linking pattern with respect to the higher level of aggregation. It seems that the new concept of a site, the presence of research groups, universities and other R&D related institutions on the Internet provide the best basis for analysis.

Scientometrics have now a whole new field of study, one that offers us the possibility to integrate different aspects of the socio-cognitive activity of science and its relationship with technology transfer. We must integrate the electronic network reality in our model for information flow among scientists, detect the links that consolidate collaborations, devise means of understanding the practices of these global scientific communities, establish relevant indicators for the socio-cognitive activity taking place on the internet and, finally, embody our results into policy recommendations.

Scientometric methodologies rest on the assumption that traces of communicated information can be used to map the development of the science system in interaction with its (social, economic, political and technological) environment. These communications can be studied in three different dimensions. The strucure of the communication networks can be mapped by quantifying the number and direction of the existing relations in the network. What is communicated can be represented (to a certain extent) by mapping title-words, key-words, etc. The role and behaviour of the persons and institutes involved in the communication can be studied as a third dimension through surveys, log-files, browsing patterns, etc.

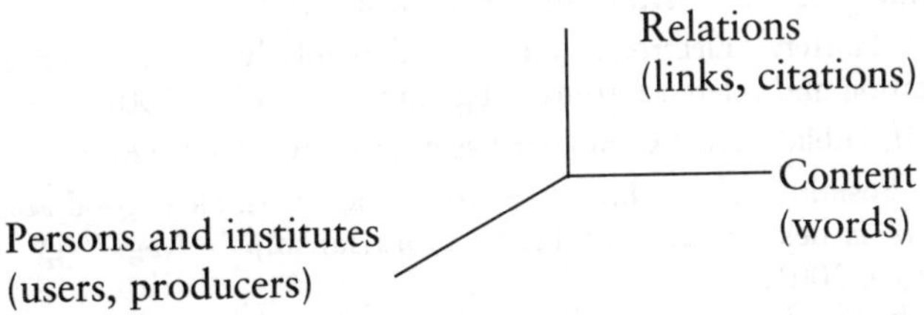

The various methodological dimensions of scientometric and webometric analysis

The relations-axis represents the type (cited reference, hyperlink) and quantity of relations between actors. The content-axis represents the 'cognitive' dimensions of communications (title-words, free-text words) and makes it possible to position the various actors in the communication networks.

A number of topics will be selected that represent the various aspects of scientific-governmental-industrial interactions and their public interface. First, a list of relevant actors will be selected. A number of analysis will be carried out that inform us about the situation in one or more of the dimensions mentioned above. A multi-layered self-organizing maps approach will be used to combine the information.

NOTES

1. Prit Chand. "Statistical bibliography or bibliometrics" *Jrl. of Documentation*. 1969; pp. 348-349.
2. D. Price. "Little Science, Big Science." N.York: Columbia Univ. Press, 1969; pp. 31-37.
3. Michael Callen. "Mapping the dynamics of Science & Technology". Sociology of Science in the real world. London: Macmillan, 1997; pp. 19-34.
4. Jeremy Rifkin. "The age of Access: The new culture of hypercapitalism. Where all of life is a paid-for-experience." *Putnam*, 2000; pp. 111-117.
5. A.F.J. Van Raan. "Bibliometrics and Internet: some observations and expectations." *Scientometrics*. 50, 2001; pp. 59-63.
6. L. Bjorneborn. "Perspectives of Webometrics." Abgefragt am. 19.11. 2001; pp. 37-38.
7. P. Ingwersen. "Data set isolation for bibliometric online analysis of research publications". *Jrl. of Ame. Society for Inf. Sc.* 48, 3, 1997; pp. 205-217.
8. D. Gibson. "Inferring web communities from link topology." ACM conference on hypertext and hypermedia. 1998.
9. S.P. Harter. "Electronic journal and scholarly communication, a citation and reference study. Abgefragt am." 15.10.2001.
10. *Ibid*. Public Access Computer System Review. 7.5.1996.
11. M. Fosmire. "Free scholarly electronic journals. How good are the two Issues in Sc. & Tech. Librarianship." Abgefragt am. 19.10. 2001.
12. D. Turnbull. "Bibliometrics and world wide web." Abgefragt am. 17.10.2001.

13. S.E. Cozzens. "What do citations count" *Scientometrics.* 15; pp. 437-447.
14. R.R. Larson. Bibli.

11

Webometrics

Library and information science is concerned with how different information resources and information structures are generated, organized, distributed and utilized by different users in different contexts. Core research area is document, which is information carrier containing text, graphics, audio, video, etc. Document representations like bibliographical data and metadata, and relations between the documents or document representation like links, cross references, citations, co-citations, bibliographic couplings. World Wide Web constitutes a research area being a document network with document in the shape of web pages interlinked by links into a hypertext structure.

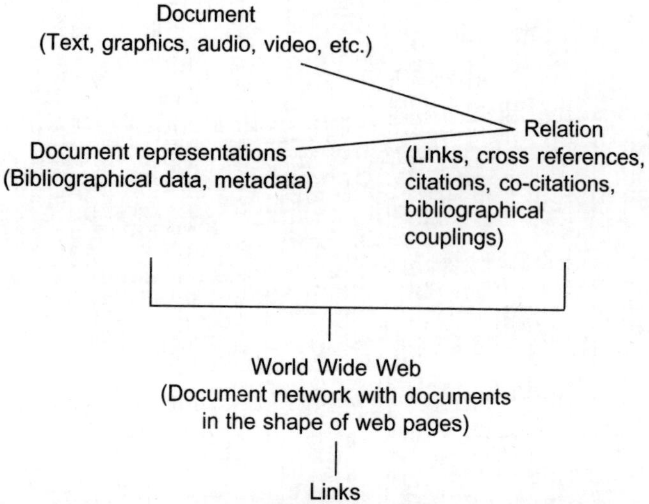

Figure: 1

World Wide Web (www) is an internet based hypertext system launched in 1991. It was an internal internet for researchers. It was used as inter-varsity computer network in 1969. www was used freely by non-CERN individuals, institutions and companies worldwide in 1993. Later www evolved from the small initial hypertext project into the largest repository and richest source of information and misinformation. The web is the fastest growing medium ever with extended technology in broader social interest. The web thus proliferated into all spheres of human enterprise as a medium for social, cultural, political, economic and scientific interaction. Now this local global document network probably contains well over five billion web pages.[1]

11.1 Self-organizing Web

The web has become a highly complex and dynamic media of diversity of information carriers for diversity of purposes. Thus web integrates all types of knowledge organization and information findings. Web could be characterized as 3D—(1) distributed (2) diversified (3) dynamic. Hypermedial documents (containing text, graphics, audio, video, etc.) are distributively located on millions of web servers. The contents and link targets of web pages reflect the immense diversity of human enterprises interests (commercial, commodities, pornographic material). Dynamic is concerned with the continuous changes and mutual adaptations of online and links across the web.

Though web system is less controlled and coordinated yet it does not mean that it is totally chaotic or unordered. On the other hand it has a link structure that reflects topic focused web clusters of interlinked web pages and web sites of researchers and their projects, papers and institutions. The web is thus similar to complex social networks.[2]

11.2 Web Graph

Researches from the field of computer science, physics, maths and information scientists have applied methods of graph theory and social network analysis to treat the web as a so-called directed graph consisting of nodes (or vertices) in the shape of web pages or websites connected by directed edges (or arcs) in the shape of directed hyperlinks.

11.2.1 Webometrics

Library and Information Science and other disciplines like science and technology, etc. have developed many systems and devices as to how the information is generated, organized, distributed and utilized by different users in different contexts. The development took place during the first half of the 20th century. It was a statistical study of bibliographies and scientific journals. The important studies were bibliometric power laws like Lotka's Law on productivity distribution among scientists, Bradford's law on the scattering of literature on a particular topic over different journals Zipf's law of word frequency in texts.[3]

Citation indexing in Science was an important development of bibliometrics and scientometrics. Access to online citation databases made effective the citation studies especially growth, diffusion, specialization, collaboration, impact and obsolescence of literature and concepts. The breakthrough of online citation analysis parallels the later avalanche of webometric studies enabled by access to large-scale web data.[4] Further, the central bibliometric measures of co-citation and bibliographic coupling (action in joining two things) have been applied to studies of web clustering, web growth and web searching.

Web has been widely used in both formal and informal scholarly communication and collaboration. Thus webometrics offers potentials for tracking (old path) aspects of scientific success traditionally more hidden from bibliometric or scientometric studies such as research results in teaching but also the actual use of scientific web pages. Webometrics and cybermetrics are the synonymous terms widely used.

11.2.2 Webometrics and bibliometrics

Global document network is now inhabited by a diversity of users. The web constitutes an obvious research field for bibliometrics, scientometrics and informatics.

Web embracing for main areas:

(i) Web page content analysis

(ii) Web link structure analysis

(iii) Web usage analysis (e.g. Log files of users' searching)

(iv) Web technology analysis (search engine performance)

The topology includes hybrid form, e.g.

(i) Web analysis techniques for automatic categorisation utilizing link graph topology.

(ii) Text contents and metadata similarly, as well as usage data.

Cybermetrics is proposed as a generic term for "The study of the quantitative aspects of the construction and use of information resources, structures and technologies on the whole internet, drawing on bibliometric and informetric approaches." Besides covering all computer-mediated communication using internet applications, it also covers quantitative measures of the internet backbone technology, topology and traffic. The coverage of cybermetrics and webometrics overlaps with proliferating computer science based approaches in analysis of web contents, link structure, web usage, and web technologies.

Thus, the term webometrics denotes a close lineage to bibliometrics and informatics. Informatics is "the study of the quantitative aspect of information in any form, not just records or bibliographics". It is "the study of quantitative aspects of production, dissemination and use of recorded information", and scientometrics is "the study of the quantitative aspects of science as a discipline or economic activities".

Webometrics includes many and large number of things by bibliometrics, because web documents, whether text or multimedia, are recorded information stored on web servers.[5] This recording may be temporary only, just as not all paper documents are properly achieved. Webometrics is partially covered by scientometrics, i.e. non-recorded material, like person-to-person conversation.

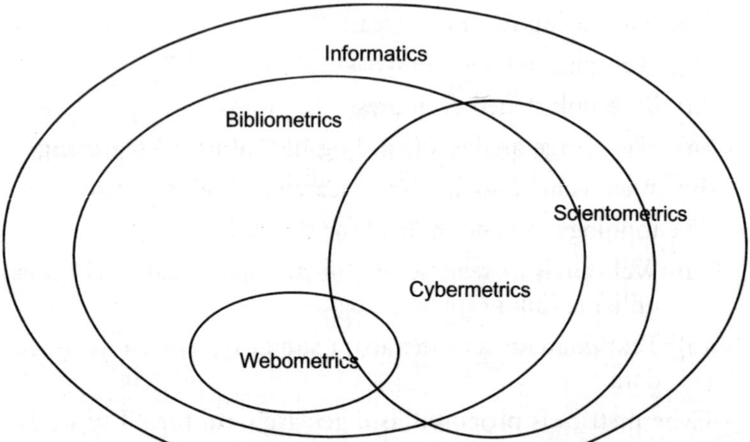

Figure: 2[6]

1. Webometrics is entirely encompassed by bibliometrics.
2. The field of cybermetrics exceeds the boundaries of bibliometrics as some activities in cyberspace normally are not recorded, but communicated synchronously (happening and existing at the same time), like in chat rooms.
3. Informatics.

Concept

Webometrics lead to a variety in the terminology. For instance, a link received by a web node. Node (A stem from which a branch grows) denotes a unit of analysis like a web page, directory or website, e.g. incoming link, inbound link, inward link, back link, and situation.

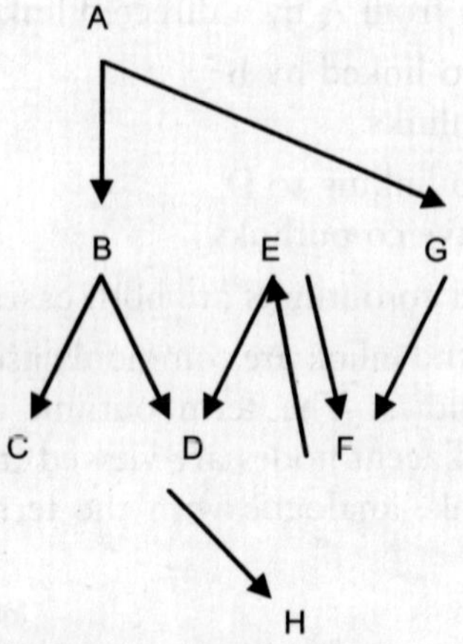

Figure: 3[7]

- B has an inlink from A
  B is inlink
  A is interlinking
  A is an in neighbor of B
- B has an outlink to C
  B is outlinking
  C is outlinking
  C is an out neighbor of B
- B has a selflink
  B is selflinking
- A has no inlinks
  A has non-linking
- C has outlinks
  C is non-linking
- I has neither in nor out links
  I is isolated
- E and F have reciprocal links
  E and F are reciprocally linked
- D, E and F have in or out links connecting each other
  They are radically interlinked
- A has a transversal outlink to G: Functioning as a shortcut

- H is reachable from A by a directed link path
- C and D are co-linked by B
  C has co-inlinks
- B and E are co-linking to D
  B and E have co-outlinks
- Co-inlinks and co-outlinks are both cases of co-links

The terms outlink and inlink are commonly used in computer science based web studies. The term outlink implics that a directed link and its adjacent nodes are viewed from the source node providing the link, analogue with the term reference in bibliometrics.

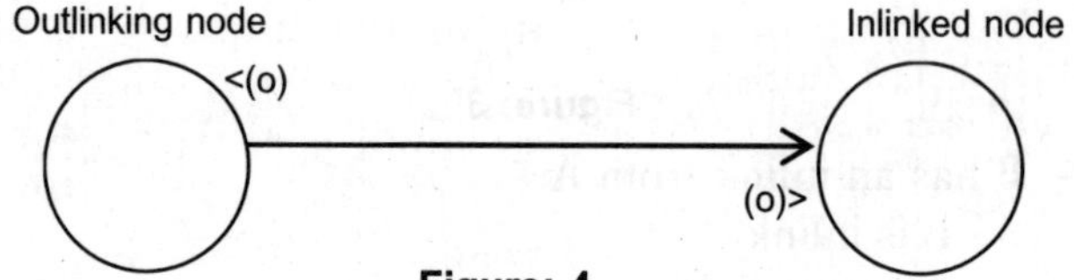

Figure: 4

The terms out neighbor and in neighbor are also used in graphic theoretical web research.

On the web, selflinks are used for a wider range of purposes than self-citations in scientific literature. Page selflinks point

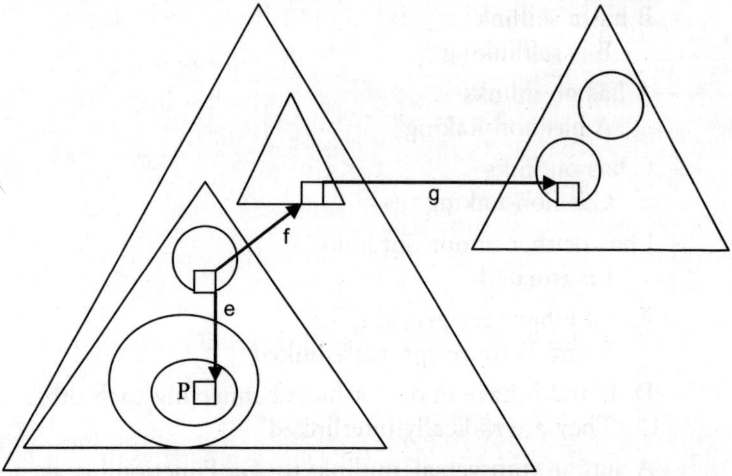

Figure: 5 Web node framework

from one section to another within the same page. Site selflink (internal links) are pointer from one page to another within the same website.

11.3 Academic Websites

Barmers Lee developed www as a global platform for interlinking academic research by facilitating researcher's information sharing through easy access to online publishing and browsing. Thus, the web also reflects and facilitates the scholarly activities. Web provides a richer and more easily accessible as well as more diversified, muddled and chattered picture of scholars' scholarly and non-scholarly activities than print media do:

- Curriculum vitae:[8]
  1. Personal research interests and profiles.
  2. Ongoing, finished or planned research projects.
  3. Links to work in progress.
  4. Book mark lists.
- Personal hobby, interests

  Family relations, friends, etc.

Academic websites are populated bypages designed for a mixture of purposes. Univesity websites function as a tool for communication, providing access, and promotion targeted at variety of users, both internal and external. The latter audience includes prospective students, staff, other academics, alumni, news media, donors/benefactors, and legislators. In a random sampling survey of 414 inter-university links from the academic web space, i.e. .ac.uk domain, over 90% of the links were created for broadly scholarly reasons, including teaching activities.

11.4 Academic Web Spaces

It was realized that quantitative methods originally designed for bibliometric analysis of citation patterns of scientific journal articles could be applied to the web by using commercial search engines to provide the raw data. It is further added that a considerable number of research articles have been published concerning scholarly communications on the web, mostly originating in the hope that web links could be used to provide similar information to that extracted from journal citations. The major difference between the two is that journal citations occur in referred documents and therefore their production is subject to quality control and they are part of the mainstream of academic endeavour, whereas hyperlinks are none of these things.

Therefore, library scientists introduced an important methodological improvement for webometric investigations of academic web spaces, for collecting primary web data directly from the investigated academic websites, instead of having to rely on secondary data collected in the big commercial search engines with opaque coverage, update frequency, indexing rules, computing performance and ranking algorithms. This created interest in the web of webometric research, especially into links in academic web spaces.

11.4.1 Geographical factors

Geographical factors for interlinking in academic web spaces have also been investigated. For example, the degree interlinking between pair of U.K. Universities decreases with geographic distance.

There are four main ADMs in use—the page, directory, domain and site. When counting objects on the web, a decision must be made about what is most appropriate unit of counting. In order to select, sample, filter, quantity and investigate different units of analysis on the web.

Thelwell introduced "Alternative Document Models" (ADM) so far particularly applied in academic web spaces as aggregated unit of analysis. There are four main ADMs in use:[9]

1. Page ADM
2. Directory ADM
3. Domain ADM
4. Site ADM

1. Page ADM is default unit consisting of individual files on the web server.
2. In Directory ADM all pages in the same web server directory identified through the URL file name path, are counted as unit.
3. Domain ADM corresponding to a subsite as ecs.soton.ac.uk (Fig. 5)—aggregated (Fig. 3) all pages with the same domain name in their URL into a common unit of analysis.
4. Site ADM (originally called University ADM) aggregates all derivative domain names into a single unit of analysis by specifying only the domain name ending.

11.4.2 Counting documents or links

The ADM models give the option to count at different aggregation level of both sources and target wage pages, each of which corresponds to a URL segmentation strategy.

The ADM models have been useful for circumventing anomalies in link data and conceptual problem with counting pages. Adamic and Huberman studied a crowl of 260000 web sites each representing a separate domain name. Two sites were considered connected if any of the pages at one site linked to any page in the other. They found that the distribution of inlinks between the sites followed a power law.

11.4.3 Academic web space and scientific journals

Another important evolving webometric research area in academic web spaces is concerned with scientific journals available on the web, also known as e-journals. Since much of webometrics has been motivated by citation analysis, a natural step has been to see if the kinds of techniques that are applied to journals and authors could also be applied to e-journal.

Vaughan and Shaw investigated Direct Web citations between scientific papers using google to collect web citation data to 46 LIS journal, the authors found predominantly significant correlations with traditional citations suggesting that online and offline citation impact are similar phenomena. A classification of 854 web citations to papers in LIS journals indicated that many web citations represented intellectual impact, covering from other papers posted on the web (30%) or from class reading lists (12%).

11.4.4 Graph theory

Today Graph theory has developed a large mathematical framework useful in a wide variety of scientific disciplines for mathematical modeling of networks, for instance, in Biology, Chemistry, Physics, Sociology, Psychology and technology. Graph theory is also applied in information sciences for modeling and analyzing, for instance, citation networks, information systems, intertextual networks, hypertextual networks.

11.5 International Network

There is still lack of research in LIS and their possible usabilities regarding different types of nodes and relations in informational network such as:

1. Web
2. Bibliographic
3. Citation networks
4. Semantic networks
5. Thesauri

Nodes in informational network are defined as corresponding either to documents, document aggregations, e.g. journals, web directories, websites), terms, authors, scientific domains (areas), institutions, or countries, etc. Distance reducing, small-world creating relations correspond to either references, citations, outlinks, inlinks, bibliographic couplings, co-cited authors, documents or journals, co-links, co-authors, cross-institutional collaborations, related terms, co-term occurrences, descriptors, etc.

Nodes and relations in International networks

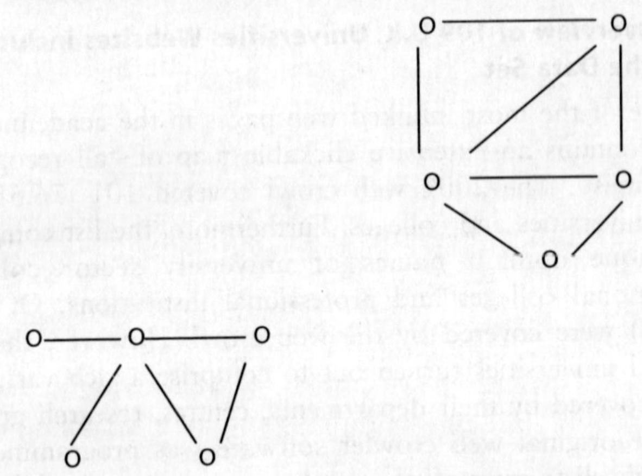

Nodes	Relations
- Author, document, document aggregations	- References, citations, outlinks /inlinks
- Authors, documents, document aggregations	- Bibliographic coupling, co-outlinks
- Author, documents, document aggregations	- Co-citations, co-links
- Author	- Co-authorship
- Terms	- Co-cited journals
- Journals	-

Aggregation—Total amount of small amounts

Universities

Times Higher Education Supplement (U.K.) has included all universities and 108 higher education institutions with special section on league tables 2001. The list includes all official U.K. universities and most of largest number of university institutions. Open universities have been omitted as the study was aimed at full time students. In order to include all large universities of U.K. in the web crowl Dr. Thelwell included the open university as web crowl. Thus, a total of 109 universities and other higher education institutions were included in 2001 web crowl.

11.6 Overview of 109 U.K. Universities Websites included in the Data Set

One of the most inlinked web pages in the academic web space contains an extensive clickable map of "all recognized universities". The 2001 web crowl covered 101 (76.5%) of these universities and colleges. Furthermore, the list comprises 74 unique domain names of university sector colleges, international colleges and professional institutions. Of these (10.8%) were covered by the web crowl. However, the 109 included universities turned out to comprise a rich variety of topics covered by their departments, centres, research groups, etc. The original web crowler software was programmed by Dr. Thelwell to start off the top homepage of each of the 109 universities, then follow all links from page to page on each university website. Some university sites had no embedded links on the web crowler. In order to allow a web crowl to take place on such sites, an alternative web page was selected as the starting point for the crowl, usually a page with a list of links to the department homepage of the university.

There may be some data problems in the original data set with regard to the included subsites. Some of the data problems were due to the circumstances that the purpose of the original link data set was to investigate corrections between inlinks counts and research assessments of universities.

While analyzing the link counts there are chances that 'non-clickable' links reflect intentions by page authors and hence should not be filtered from the data set. Link should be valid and 'clickable'. If they are not valid and 'clickable' they do not allow web crowlers or web surfers to access target web pages.

NOTES

1. I.F. Aguillo. "STM information on the web and the development of new internet R&D databases and indicators". *Online Information. Prcgs*. 1998; pp. 239-243.
2. L. Adamio and E. Adar. "Friends and neighbours on the web". *Social Networks*. 25(3); pp. 211-236.

3. R. Larson. "Bibliometrics of the WWW." *Procg. of ASIS*, 1996; pp. 71-78.
4. R.H. Abraham. "Webometry: Measurement and complexity of WWW." Visual Math Insti., Univ. of California at Santa Cruz. 1996.
5. Chakraborti (et al). "The structure of broad topics on the web Minings the web links structure." IEEE Computer. 32, 8; pp. 60-67.
6. J. Tague-Sutcliffe. "An introduction to informatics." *Inf. Processing & Management*. 28, 1; pp. 1-3.
7. L. Bjornborn. "Perspectives of Webometrics." *Scientometrics*. 50, 1; pp. 65-82.
8. P. Ingwersen. "The calculation of web impact factors." *Jrl. of Documentation*, 54, 2; pp. 236-243.
9. V. Cano and N.C. Lind. "Citation. Life cycles of tex citation classics" *Scientometrics*. 43, 1, pp. 77-85.

Open Access to Users in Information System

12

In the past, access to information in various higher institutions was reserved for a relatively small number of administrators. Open access is even considered beneficial for providing information to users. The demand is slow because of defaults in organizational structures, including the natural division between academic and administrative computing as well as management issues, principally serious security considerations. The user information system widely serves the need of every one. User information system includes transaction system as well as high level office efficiency and information sharing. This increases productivity and service by adding value in the form of new features to current systems.

12.1 Implementation

It is necessary to adopt an overall system and approach to data administration and management that will provide a platform for universal and secure access to campus information. This concept helps a foundation to enable an institute to make a smooth transition to new technologies in their development and availability through primary and secondary data technology. It will need changes in hardware and software tools from time to time, but the data requirement for completeness and consistency across all systems will remain constant. One constant is data which are never obsolete.

This system was first implemented in Boston College from a batch processing made to an outline interactive system. It needs to establish a framework that will facilitate transition.

The first was the Apple Macintosh in 1984 as it was easy for use-to-use graphic interface, its desktop metaphore, and the consistency of the interface across all applications. The second was the use of voice for registration of students.

12.2 Traditional Environment

Term such as 'stable', 'reliable', 'secure', 'closed', 'procedural', and integrated are often attributed to mainframe based administrative system. But the ultimate measurement is not whether data are distributed or centrally stored, or whether the user interface is intuitive or whether the applications are creative or rather, whether system is reliable. Four major issues inherent in the traditional information systems environment have played a key role in effecting the progress by taking advantage of technology.

There is lack of clarity between control and management, control of data and information should always be in the hands of the users but the responsibility of management should be in the hands of the information system professionals.

There are two factors—centralization and decentralization. The physical decentralization of hardware, data and other sources is one aspect of the issue. It is as if campus users believe they will get better service when they have better control over programming staff. But, often it is a short-term benefit. For institutions that have taken the approach of allowing everyone to define everything they want—an individual processor, an enormous infrastructure of bridges, gateways, translators, and converters will eventually and inevitably be needed. However, an important way for computer professionals to develop a global systems perspective is to have involvement in all sort of different activities and systems and not be pigeonholed. There should be a central computing and communication management, and like any other activity, planning for transition is the key. Centralised planning is a key factor in the design of a campus wide system that will support the concept of openers. Centralised management database is necessary to provide a high degree of referential integrity which ensures the validity of shared data. Control belongs to users, planning is a joint effort, and management of environment is the responsibility of the information system staff.

12.3 User Involvement

It is not advisable to involve user in management/ administrative system. He should think about new ways of doing things and to exchange ideas with the information technology staff. A user gains technological expertise and acquires individual power. It is not uncommon for a user to become expert in a particular software package, and then to advocate the virtues of the product. For information systems to make a difference, there is a need for a high level of commitment for both the user department and information system management.

12.4 Intelligent and Intuitive System

The intelligence of a system comes from a permanency of the underlying structure of the institution. In its simplest form, an educational institution is composed of a set of buildings, where courses are taught, search is conducted and students live, and a collection of positions that are filled by individuals who teach, research, answer telephones, operate computers and so on. The brick and mortar of the buildings, the faculty and employee positions, and the organizational structure are the aspects of the environment which are permanent. These are the things people move in and out of. They have relationship with each other when someone joins the campus as a student or a professional.

The major player in this new environment is the library. One of the many roles of the library is to provide access to information being managed within the same structure as access to library material.[1] After all, library clients—faculty students and staff—are the same customers being served not only by a policy of open access to administrative information, but free access as well. By providing free and open access libraries, they encourage the use of available facilities, rather than inhibiting usage by charging fees. Many computing and communications interfaces have gained the label 'intuitive' not only because of their so-called 'ease of use' but also because of the acceptance that commonly-used interfaces have acquired through broad exposure. For example, the telephone has been an accepted medium for a long time, but we have all now embraced a new variety of other devices as well, such as telephone.[2]

The other characteristic of access control is the number levels needed for particular activities. There are four parts to access control: authentication, identification, encryption and location. For instance, it is not necessary to know the location of someone accessing him or her electronic mail messages and in some cases, even the use of a password is not necessary. Library catalog information may be accessed by anyone, even someone not identified as holding an institutional position. The nature of the information should dictate the necessary levels of access control.

The system should be able to control access to information and only deliver legitimate functions to users, but the ability of users to customize menus is essential. The information resources should be viewed as a smorgasbord, so that users can pick and choose the items that are most important, and arrange the presentation to meet their specific needs. Users should also be free to not choose available services as menu items.

Example: Users to access information systems

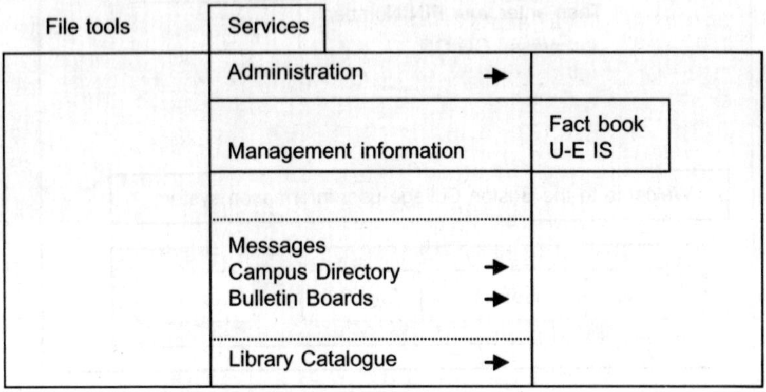

Boston College Information System

Trying to format a standard set of menu functions and information sources for all individuals or class of individuals is not the solution. For example, one user may want access to a full range of information resources in a disaggregated form, while another executive of the same level may only want to see a limited set of standard reports on a regular schedule. The only reasonable solution is to permit access, under proper controls, to whatever is available, and to allow the individual to customize even his or her menu.

12.5 ID Cards

As soon as an individual is identified through the transactional system as being associated with the institution/library as a student/user, user information service (UIS) automatically generates identification information. Usually, the first action of a new student is to obtain a university ID card, which contains a unique bar-code label and an encoded magnetic stripe. This card works as passport that has usage in library as well as campus.

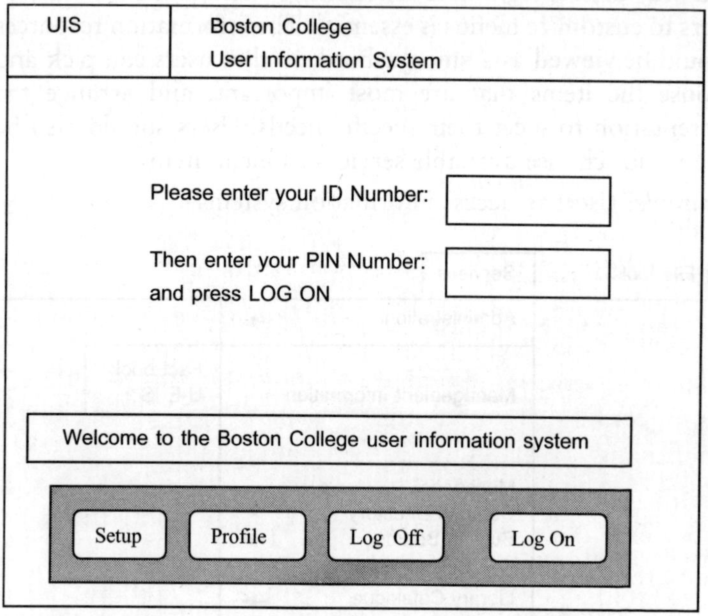

Common Log-on procedure allows access by ID Number

When the university ID card is issued, the user information system also automatically generates a unique username, password, and PIN for each individual. The changing of passwords on a regular basis is one of the standard controls in most security systems. The concept of the PIN also differs from passwords in another significant way, just as the student, faculty members, will use the same ID card to access many application systems, the individual will also always use the same PIN.

NOTES

1. Peter F. Drucker. *The Frontiers of Management*. New York: Truman Tally, 1986.
2. F.B. Campawell. Boston College, "Strategic plan for computing and communications." Boston College, 1986; p. 1.

Greenstone: A Software for Digital Library

13

13.1 Introduction

Greenstone is a suite of software for building and distributing digital library collections. It provides a new way of organizing information and publishing it on the Internet or on CD-ROM. It is produced by the New Zealand Digital Library Project at the university of Waikato and developed and distributed in co-operation with UNESCO under the GNU General Public License. It is a suite software and capable to serve digital library collection and build new collections. It is a cooperative effort and the readers' interface is available in 38 languages.

13.2 Aims

The aim of Greenstone software is to empower users, particularly in university libraries and other public service institutions.

1. It builds its own digital libraries. Digital libraries are radically reforming how information is disseminated and acquired in UNESCO's partner communities and institutions in the fields of education, science and culture around the world, and particularly in developing countries.
2. This software will encourage the effective deployment of digital libraries to share information for the benefit of the society.
3. It provides a new way of organising information and publishing it on the internet in the form of a fully searchable metadata.

13.3 Operating Elements

It is open source, multilingual software, issued under the terms of GNU 'General Public License.'

13.4 Platforms

Greenstone runs on all versions of Windows and UNIX and Mac OS-X. It is very easy to install. For the default Windows installation absolutely no configuration is necessary and end-users routinely install Greenstone on their personal main web server, where it interpolates with standard web server software (e.g. Apache).

13.5 Interoperability

Greenstone is highly interoperable using contemporary standard[1]. It incorporates a server that can serve any collection over the open archives protocol for metadata harvesting (OAI-PMH). GREENSTONE can harvest documents over OAI-PMH and include them in a collection. Any collection can be exported to METS and Greenstone can ingest documents in METS form. Any collection can be exported to D space ready for D space's batch import program, and any D space collection can be imported into Greenstone.

13.6 Interfaces

Greenstone has two separate interactive interfaces: (i) reader interface in which the end users access the digital library through the reader interface, which operates within a web browser, (ii) the librarian interface which is Java-based graphical user interface that makes it easy to gather material for a collection and enriches it by adding metadata, design the searching and browsing facilities that the collection will offer the user, and serve the collection.

13.7 Metadata Formats

Users define metadata interactively within the librarian inerface. These metadata sets are predefined.

- Dublin core (qualified and unqualified).
- RFC 1807.
- NZGLS (New Zealand Government Locator Service).

- AGLS (Australian Government Locator Service) New metadata sets can be defined using Greenstone's metadata set editor "Plug-ins" are used to ingest externally prepared metadata in different forms and plug-ins exist for.
- XML, MARC, CDS/ISIS, precut, Bibtex, Refer, OAI, D space, METS.

13.8 Document Format

Plug-ins are also used to ingest documents for textual documents. There are plug-ins for PDF, Post Script, Word, RTF, HTML, Plain Text, Latex, Z1 Parchive & Excel, PPT, E-mail and source code. For multimedia documents, there are 'plug-ins' for images (any format, including GIF, JIF, JPEG, TIFF), MP3 Audio, Ogg Vorbis audio and a generic plug-in that can be configured for audio formats, MPEG, MIDJ, etc.

13.9 User Base

It is distributed on source forge, a leading distribution centre for open source software:

Distributed via Source forge since	:	Nov. 2000
Average Downloads since then	:	4500/Month
Current running at	:	4500/Month

Proportion of downloads that are documentation: 60%

Proportion of downloads that are software : 40%

Of these, 80% are Windows binaries

15% are Linux binaries

5% are source

13.10 Distribution

Digital libraries use multiple computers typically for storage. Libraries share files with another library so that information may be protected from fire, earthquake or erasure—accidental or malicious and can be received from the other site.

13.11 Open Source and Proprietary Systems

In the early days, hardware was so expensive that software costs hardly seemed to matter. Software normally ran one kind of hardware. Today all has changed. Much software runs on multiple platforms. The best known open source system is the Linux operating system and competes with both Microsoft Windows and various favors of Unix.[2] Perhaps more important to the digital library community is the Greenstone open source package in multiple languages and multiple platforms like Linux. Greenstone code is open and available for inspection or use without charge. Greenstone provides many facilities:

Greenstone enables users to build digital library collection and make them accessible to user either locally on CD-ROM or over the web.

It includes text search image display hierarchical browsing fielded data and many other capabilities.

13.12 Greenstone and the Web

Greenstone provides information just by "putting it on the web". The information becomes searchable, browsable and maintainable, in the following manner:

(a) Each collection, prior to presentation, undergoes a "building" process that, once established, is fully automatic. 1. Witter I.H., Moffat, A. and Bell, T.C. (1999) Managing gigabytes: Compressing and indexing documents and images. Morgan Kufmann, San Francisco, C.A. 1999.

(b) Searching utilises various indexes to text and/or metadata, while browsing utilises metadata such as title and author.

(c) Greenstone supports collections in many different languages.

13.13 Searching

Fulltext searching depends on the collection user select indexes built from different parts of the full text or the metadata. Some collections have separate indexes of full documents, sections, paragraphs, title and section headings, each of which can be searched for particular words and phrases. When browsing the user examines data structures created from metadata the list of authors, title, dates, hierarchical classification structure for both searching and browsing are specified by instructions configuration file, and can be rebuilt entirely automatically. No information is inserted by hand.

Each document may be hierarchically organised into logical sections each of which comprises paragraph metadata such as author, title, date, keywords may be associated with documents with individual sections. This is raw material for indexes.

(A) GREENSTONE COLLECTOR: It is an interactive system for managing and accessing collections. The collector can be used to:

(a) Create a new collection with the same structure as an existing one.

(b) Create a new collection with a different structure.

(c) Add new material to an existing collection.

(d) Modify the structure of an existing collection.

(e) Delete a collection.

(f) Write an existing collection to a self-contained self-installing Windows CD-ROM.

(B) DIALOG STRUCTURE: Upon completion of login, a new page appears that shows the sequence of the following steps involved in collection building:

(a) Collection information.

(b) Source data.

(c) Configuring the collection.

(d) Viewing the collection.

(a) Collection Information: It is the first step. Collection development is to enter some information about the new collection. The title is a short phrase used to identify the collection. The user also enters that text which appears under the collection.

(b) Source Data: The second step is that user specifies the source text that comprises the collection. The user chooses which collection is cloned from a pull-down menu. Many Greenstone installations have several different collections. The document the file types is the new collection which should be amongst those in the one being cloned. The same metadata should be available, and the metadata should be specified in the same way.

When creating a completely new collection, a bland collection configuration file is provided that accepts most document types and generates a searchable index of the full text and a title browsers since this metadata is normally available. Boxes are provided to indicate where the source documents are located. Any number of input sources can be specified. Specification can be:

(a) a directory name on the Greenstone server system (beginning with "file://").

(b) an address beginning with "http://" for files to be downloaded from the web.

(c) an address beginning with "ftp://" for files to be downloaded using FTP.

(c) **Configuring and Collection:** The construction and presentation of all collections are controlled by the specifications in a configuration file. Advanced users may use the next page to alter the settings in this file.

(a) The building stage is where the action takes place.

(b) First the internal name is chosen for the collection, based on the title that has been supplied.

(c) Then the directory structure is created that includes sub-directories to receive, index and present the source documents.

(d) A recursive file system copy command is issued to retrieve source documents ready on the file system.

(e) For offset files a web mirroring package is used to copy the specified site along with any related image file.

Next: The documents are covered into a standard XML form. Appropriate plug-ins to perform this operation must be specified in the collection configuration file.

(g) Then the full text searching indexes and browsing structure specified in the collection configuration file are created.

(h) Finally the result of the building process is moved to the area for active collection.

However, Greenstone provides:

1. Flexible searching
2. Flexible browsing
3. Zero maintenance
4. Phrases and Key phrases[3]
5. Sustained operation
6. Multimedia
7. CD-ROM options
8. Distributed collections[4]

13.14 Conclusion

Greenstone is an open source software. It is easily modified. Greenstone is widely accessible through a standard web browser. Collection can be served on Windows or Unix, with an external web server or a built-in one. Browsing indexes are built from metadata. Plug-ins can be written to accommodate new document types. Classifiers can be written to create new kinds of browsing indexes based on metadata. The interface is available in multiple languages. Collection containing millions of documents and up to several gigabytes have been built. Full text searching is fast. The Z 39.50 protocol is supported for accessing internal servers and for presenting Greenstone collection to external servers. Its developers received 2004 IFIP Namur awards for "contribution to the awareness of social implication of information technology and the need for a holistic approach in the use of information technology that takes account of social implications".

APPENDIX—I

Institutions applied public Greenstone collection:

1. Association of Indian Labour Historians, Delhi
2. Auburn University, Alabama
3. California University at Riverside
4. Chicago University Library
5. Detroit Public Library

6. Gresham College, London
7. Hawaiian Electronic Library
8. Illinois Wesleyan University
9. Indian Institute of Management
10. Kyrgyz Republic National Library
11. Le High University, Pennsylvania
12. Mari El Republic, Russia
13. National Centre for Science Information, Bangalore, India
14. Netherlands Institute for Scientific Information Services
15. New York Botanical Garden
16. Peking University Digital Library
17. Philippine Research Education and Government Information Network
18. Secretary of Human Rights of Argentina
19. Slavonski Brod Public Library, Slovenia
20. State Library of Tasmania
21. Stuttgart University of Applied Sciences
22. Texas A&M University Center for the Study of Digital Libraries
23. University of Illinois
24. University of North Carolina Ibiblio Project
25. Vietnam National University
26. Vimercte Public Library, Milan, Italy
27. Washington Research Library Consortium
28. Welsh Books Council

UN Agencies

1. UNESCO, Paris—
   Sponsors distribution of the Greenstone software as part of its Information for All programme.
2. Food and Agriculture Organization (FAO), Rome—
   Its Information Management Resource Kit uses Greenstone as the (only) example of digital library

software in the Digitization and digital libraries self-instructional module.

3. Institute for Information Technology in Education (IITE), Moscow—
   Has commissioned an extensive course on Digital libraries in education and uses Greenstone for all the practical work.
   United Nations University (UNU), Japan—
   Two CD-ROM collections of UNU material have been produced.

HUMANITARIAN COLLECTIONS: Greenstone is used by Human Info NGO in Belgium to produce collections of humanitarian information and distribute them on CD-ROM widely throughout the developing world. (For more information, contact Michel Loots mloots@humaninfo.org)

Number of humanitarian collections:	approx 35-40
Annual distribution of each one:	approx 5,000 copies

LANGUAGES: One of Greenstone's unique strengths is its multilingual nature. The reader's interface is available in the following languages:

* Arabic, Armenian, Bengali, Catalan, Croation, Czech, Chinese (both simplified and traditional), Dutch, English, Farsi, Finnish, French, Galician, Georgian, German, Greek, Hebrew, Hindi, Indonesian, Italian, Japanese, Kannada, Kazakh, Kyrgyz, Latvian, Maori, Mongolian, Portuguese (BR and PT versions), Russian, Serbian, Spanish, Thai, Turkish, Ukrainian and Vietnamese.

TRAINING CENTRES: Training is a bottleneck for widespread adoption of any digital library software. Many international training courses have been run.

1. **UNESCO**
   Has sponsored training courses in Bangalore (2002 and 2003), Almaty (2003), Senegal (2004), Suva (2004).
2. **Self-study Courses**
   FAO and UNESCO IITE have produced training material on Greenstone.

3. **Digital Library Conferences**
   There have been Greenstone tutorials (on several occasions) at all major digital library conferences: JCDL, ECDL, ICADL, ICDL.
4. **Librararin Conferences**
   There have been Greenstone workshops and presentations to run LITA, DLF, ALA Annual Conference.
5. **Payson Institute, Tsulane University**
   Has run courses that use Greenstone collections as a resource in locations in Africa (Burkina Faso, Cameroon, Cote d'lvoire, Democratic Republic of Congo, Ghana, Rwanda, Senegal, Sierra Leone, Togo) and Latin America (Argentina, Bolivia, Colombia, Ecuador, Guatemala).
6. **Others**
   There have been several Greenstone courses in India (e.g. Kozhikode, Pune), some in Canada (Vancouver, Calgary, Edmonton), one in Cuba (Havana).

NOTES

1. Humanity Development Library: Subject Hierarchy. http://www.nzdl.org/egibin/library ? a = d & c hdl & cl = L1.16.9.
2. I.H. Witten, D. Bainbridge and S.J. Boddie. "Power to the people: end-user building of digital library collections." Proc Joint Conference on Digital Libraries, Roanoke, VA, 2001; pp. 94-103.
3. G.W. Paynter, I.H. Witten, S.J. Cunninham and G. Buchanan (2000). "Scalable Browsing for Large Collections: a Case Study." Proc Fifth ACM Conference on Digital Libraries, San Antonio, TX, pp. 215-223; June.
4. D. Bainbridge, I.H. Witten, G. Buchanan, J. McPherson, S. Jones and A. Maahoui (2001). "Greenstone: A Platform for distributed digital library applications." Proc European Digital Library Conference, Darmstadt, Germany; September.

Application of ISO-9000 in the Libraries

14

14.1 Introduction

In the information era, to provide quality service to the users is the main objective of modern library. The ISO-9000 services of library management standards are a result of the ISO's commitment to promoting a systematic and structured approach to library management by evolving and establishing a set of international criteria.

14.2 Quality Concept

Quality is a dynamic phenomenon. It is being improved every moment with the new developments in technology and management techniques. As the leading organizations of the world improve the quality standards of their products or services, the quality expectations of the customers from other organizations also go up. In response, the number of organizations worldwide adopting new quality management techniques to keep pace with the international quality standards ISO-9000 is one of the most widely recognized quality management tools for effective quality management and for achieving greater customer satisfaction, being adopted by almost every quality conscious company of the world. ISO-9000 is a series of quality system standards formulated and published by international organization for standardization.

India is one of the founding members of ISO and participating through Bureau of Indian Standards (BIS) as an active member in various technical and management committees of ISO. Its principal objectives include formulation of national standards and certification of products and services. In order to make Indian products and services more competitive and acceptable in international market, BIS has introduced "Quality System Certification Scheme" according to ISO-14000 series of standards. These standards are adopted from ISO-9000 and are exactly similar. This scheme envisages grant of quality system certification and licence to the Indian Companies. [Ref. BIS Certification Amendment Regulations, 1991].

14.3 Elements of ISO-9001

Out of several key elements of ISO-9001 following are very important:

1. Management responsibility
2. Quality system
3. Contract review
4. Design control
5. Document control
6. Purchasing
7. Purchaser supplied product
8. Product identification and traceability
9. Process control
10. Inspection and testing
11. Inspection measuring and test equipments
12. Inspection and test status
13. Control of non-conforming products
14. Corrective action
15. Handling, storage, packaging and delivery
16. Quality records
17. Training
18. Servicing

14.4 Need of ISO in the Libraries

Like corporate sectors, now the need of ISO in libraries is well accepted. Deming's 11 points are very important in this regard.

1. Establish constancy of purpose for service improvement. Libraries should avoid short-term 'band-aid' solutions

to quality problems. Instead, long-term planning at the board and administrative levels must consider how quality service delivery can best be achieved.

2. Adopt the new quality philosophy. Those who work in libraries must adopt a philosophy in which negativism and poor service are unacceptable.
3. Cease dependence upon mass inspection. Continuous improvement, not quality assurance, is the key to excellent service. With a quality assurance approach, staff members will assume their errors will be detected by others, and thus may underemphasize the importance of doing things right the first time quality breakdown.
4. End the practice of awarding vendor business based on price alone. Rather than constantly searching for cheaper suppliers, long-term relationships should be established with vendors.
5. Improve constantly and forever every system of service. TQM is not a one-time effort, not even something that is ever accomplished. Instead, it is a journey. Because of the high level of interdependency among organizational members in a library, a team approach is required for making decisions about quality improvements.
6. Institute training procedures. Staff members often learn their jobs from colleagues who were improperly trained themselves. When this occurs, new members cannot adequately perform. Instead, organization members should receive proper training through activities such as in-services, professional conferences and continuing education.
7. Adopt and institute leadership. Leadership means discovering and removing barriers that prevent individuals from doing their work.
8. Drive out fear so that everyone can work effectively. Library staff members must feel secure if quality is to improve. They must be able to ask questions, report quality problems, and take a firm position on necessary improvements without fear of reprisal.

9. Break down barriers between departments. One department's goals can interfere with another's. Therefore, departments must be able to communicate with each other. Departmentalism must be replaced by an identification with the mission of the entire library.
10. Remove barriers that rob people of pride in workmanship. Barriers such as outdated equipment, substandard materials, and authoritarian managers stand in the way of quality improvement. Annual ratings and merit pay heighten conflict and competition. The humanity of the workforce must be fostered through true delegation and autonomy, not through pseudo-participation.
11. Create a new structure that puts everybody in the organization to work accomplishing the transformation. Administrators must communicate a new vision for the members and provide structure in which people can contribute to the quality mission.

Benefits of ISO

After obtaining ISO-9000 certificate several benefits—tangible and intangible—are seen, such as:

- customer satisfaction
- management confidence
- boosting employees' morale by involvement of every employee
- higher productivity
- higher acceptability
- higher profitability
- better access to global market.

Limitations

We have to verify whether ISO-9000 is able to answer the following points:

(a) How could we ensure the standardization for an intangible output/product?

(b) Could we standardize the learning/teaching methodology with the help of ISO-9000?

(c) How would we reach a benchmark in each individual functional area?

(d) Are the professional auditors aware of the intricacies of library operations?

TQM and Information Technology

15

The goal of the early library was to store and preserve the recorded knowledge in various formats. Librarians were more concerned with making heritage of knowledge more accessible to their readers and were less concerned with problems of preservation, communication of right information to right reader expeditiously through various methods and media. The information explosion is at its greatest like depending on more than one library, growth of literature, increase in acquisition. It has pressurized the libraries to drastically change and modify their information handling techniques[1] by:

(a) adopting more efficient techniques.

(b) cooperating sharing of resources among information centres.

(c) changing the attitude and behaviour of librarians.

The past industrial period has brought considerable advances and innovations in technology which resulted in so many new inter-disciplinary fields have emerged including information technology like:

(a) computing power into wide spectrum of information handling process.

(b) convergence of telecommunication and computer system facilities.

(c) development of wide range of equipment.

15.1 Information System

Information system involves all aspects of handling information. Bibliographic retrieval is concerned with the processing of available books and documents. Science and technology will remain the stimulus for the advancement and development of the society. The objective of science is to discover scientific truths. Both are closely linked and have been the backbone of the progress of developed nations. Information is power and helps in decision-making correctly and expeditiously.

15.1.1 Quality assurance and management

Quality means 'zero' redundancy or may be termed as product and services provided by the library or information center for use and consumption, and for treasure and creation of new information/knowledge. Quality library services play a significant role in quality education and research.

Total quality management is concerned with the integration of all efforts in the organization towards quality and customer care. It deals with continuous information, prevention rather than detecting defects, customer focus and universal responsibility. TQM in library is beneficial because users will be satisfied and better treated, excellence in library service will be achieved, better systems and procedures will be followed, substantial improvement will be visible, new organizational climate will be generated and employees will develop a sense of belonging.

Relevance of TQM and Library Services

The change in IT environment will achieve "Information for all" and "user satisfaction at optimum level". Information technologies which are relevant to libraries mainly cover the following:[2]

(a) *Computer Technology*

(i) Database organization and management.

(ii) Library base organization.

(b) *Library Technologies*

(i) Classification.

(ii) Cataloguing/indexing.

(iii) Database creation.

(iv) CAS.

(v) SDI.

(c) *Communication Technologies*

(i) Library network.

(ii) Information network.

(d) *Reprographic Technologies*

(i) Photography.

(ii) Microfilm.

(iii) Optical/Digital.

(iv) Audio/Video.

(e) *Technical Communication Technologies*

(i) Technical writing.

(ii) Editing.

(iii) Publishing.

(f) *Information Technologies Applied in Libraries*

(i) Library automation.

(ii) Information storage and retrieval.

(iii) Internet services and information network.

15.2 Essence of TQM

Library users are now demanding quality services which a library should provide. Quality and management were two separate disciplines. But management philosophy combined them, embracing all activities and practices through which the needs and expectations of the customer and the community, and the objectives of the organization, are satisfied in the most efficient and cost-effective way by maximizing the potential of all employees in a continuing drive for improvement.

The activities of TQM may be categorized as under:[3]

As of Quality in libraries

(a) Accessibility

(b) Availability

(c) Applicability

Cs of TQM

(a) Commitment

(b) Competence

(c) Continuous improvement

(d) Customer service

Cs of customer service

(a) Continuous information collection

(b) Customisation

(c) Consistency

(d) Cost and delivery

(e) Cooperation/coordination

(f) Communication

Es of TQM

(a) Efficiency

(b) Economy

(c) Effectiveness

L of TQM

(a) Leadership

M of TQM

(a) Management

Ps of TQM

(a) Performance measure/evaluation

(b) Performance standards

Ts of TQM

(a) Trust

(b) Teamwork

(c) Training

(d) Techniques

(e) Tools

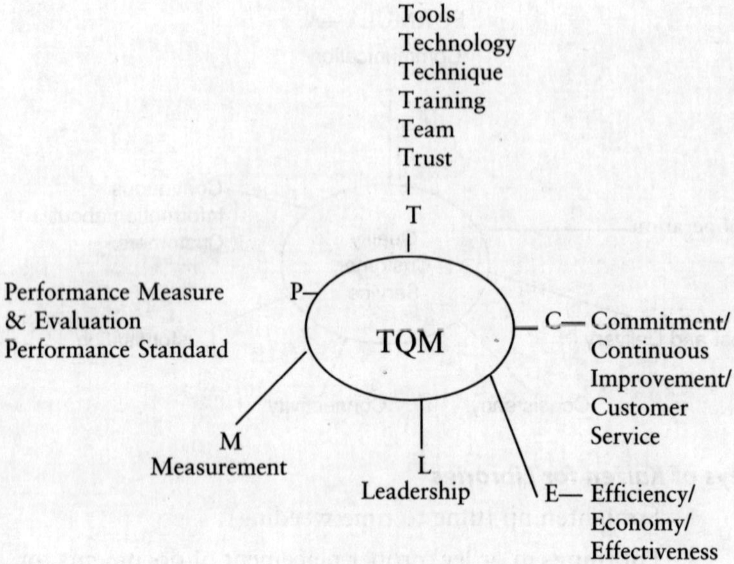

Formula—CELMPT

FORMULA—A

Keys of Kaizen for Libraries

1. Straighten up (time to time weeding)
2. Put things in order (proper placement of documents for retrieval)
3. Clean up (keep the library clean)
4. Personal cleanliness (of professional & technical staff)
5. Discipline (develop and follow Systems)

15.3 TQM in Information and IITs

Library automation system concerns all library functions, OPAC, Bar-code based circulation system, acquisition and serial access. CD-ROM network permits online access to bibliographic database throughout the campus as well as through dial up access.[4] The Home page developed information on the daily library life by promoting access points to various services.

The need for collaboration of librarians and information technologists arises from convergence of their missions, user demand for coordinated services and competition for sources. Moreover, the pace of technology requires rapid yet flexible responses, not protected haggling over territories, roles and responsibilities. In contrast, client server technologies and disputed computing requires offer of new freedom and flexibility to users but at the same time push complex technical issues and knowledge requirements outward to the desktops, librarians and end users, where the skills to cope with are often inconsistent.

(a) *Initiative Skills*

In IIT libraries the library staff has to cultivate communication skills, tact and good judgement, and the ability to create and sustain positive relations between the library and the clientele. Library professionals try to understand how to interpret and evaluate diverse sources of data.[5] The goal here is continually evolving, i.e. to continue best practices for doing research and reference work to satisfy the clients.

(b) *Networking*

IIT's libraries are special and technical libraries and work in three complementary groups of information professionals—creators, communicators and consolidators. The staff using the systems that satisfy the reader's need deliver quality. Networking plays a vital role in sharing the resources, developing the communications, reduction of costs and an environment more global in nature. LAN and WAN, internet, intranet are being adopted for development and utilization of information, in which basic components are involved, i.e. hardware, software, supplies, personnel (professional and non-professional), and installation of new technologies.

(c) *On-line search*

In IIT libraries of Delhi and Roorkee, a search request form is important starting point. Search file seat is prepared with details. Such users are known as direct users. The indirect user's request is made by past, and their link is user and searcher. With the establishment of NISSAT in 1987, the network programme came into being. IITs are linked with network programs like ERNET, INFLIBNET, DELNET, etc.

IIT libraries of Delhi and Roorkee are growing and changing very fast in their modern technologies to improve the lifestyle of the youngers by improving quality by implementing various technologies, e.g. Audio-Video technology, optical technologies, CD-ROM, Video-disk technology, satellite technology, facsimile technology, hypertext and hypermedia technology, voice mail technology, bar-code technology, etc.

Total Quality Management In Libraries

TQM is "a system of continuous improvement employing participative management and centered on the needs of customers"[6]. Key components of TQM are employee involvement and training, problem-solving teams, statistical methods, long-term goals and thinking, and recognition that the system. not people, produces inefficiencies. Libraries can benefit from TQM in three ways: (i) breaking down interdepartmental barriers; (ii) redefining the beneficiaries of library services as internal customers (staff) and external customers (patrons); and (iii) reaching a state of continuous improvement.

A library should focus on providing the best services possible, and be willing to change to serve its customers. What do the customers come in for? How can I look at the efficiency of my library? How do we serve the current customers that exist today? First learn about the customer, then solve the problems.

Steps to TQM

There are 12 steps that managers in any type of organization can take to implement a total quality management program.[7]

1. Purpose should stay for improvement of product and service. Constancy of purpose requires innovation, investment in research and education, continuous improvement of product and service, maintenance of equipment, furniture and fixtures, and new aids to production.
2. New philosophy should be adopted—management must undergo a transformation and begin to believe in quality products and services.
3. Inspect products and services only enough to be able to identify ways to improve the process.
4. The lowest priced goods are not always the highest quality; choose a supplier based on its record of improvement and then make a long-term commitment to it.
5. Improvement is not a one-time effort; management is responsible for leading the organization into the practice of continual improvement in quality and productivity.

6. Institute should organize an in-service training. Workers need to know how to do their jobs correctly even if they need to learn new skills.
7. Leadership is the job of management. Managers have the responsibility to discover the barriers that prevent staff from taking pride in what they do. The staff will know what those barriers are.
8. There should be no fear. People often fear reprisal if they "make waves" at work. Managers need to create an environment where workers can express concerns with confidence.
9. Managers should promote teamwork by helping staff in different areas/departments to work together.
10. Slogans, exhortations, and targets should be avoided for the workforce. Using slogans alone, can be offensive to workers because they imply that a better job could be done. Managers need to learn real ways of motivating people in their organizations.
11. Quotas impede quality more than any other working condition; they leave no room for improvement. Workers need the flexibility to give customers the level of service they need.
12. Pride of workmanship should not have any barrier. Give workers respect and feedback about how they are doing their jobs.

How Libraries have Improved Services with TQM

Many libraries have implemented TQM successfully. IIT Libraries created a task force which rewrote the library's vision statement, and considered changes that would have to be made in order to develop a new organization culture—one that highlights the changing nature of staff roles and responsibilities in an era of pervasive change. Its principles of service excellence, teamwork, ongoing training and skill building, process/systems focus, continuous improvement, and cooperation across boundaries could help them make the changes they needed.

Sirkin[8] (1993) suggests some ways a library might use the principles of TQM to enhance library services.

1. Create service brochures and information kits.
2. Conduct a user survey about library services.
3. Change hours of operation.
4. Provide a more convenient material return.
5. Simplify checkout of materials.
6. Cooperate with local government.
7. Give new staff a thorough orientation.
8. Create interdepartmental library advisory groups.
9. Improve the physical layout of the library.
10. Develop an active outreach program.
11. Publicize new or changed services.
12. Develop user and staff training materials.
13. Offer electronic document delivery.
14. Follow the mission statement.
15. Smile.

Potential Challenges

There are four barriers to the adoption of TQM in libraries: (1) vocabulary: objections to terms such as "total", "quality" and "management" which imply that high standards are not already being met; (2) commitment: TQM takes several years to implement and requires a long-term commitment by library managers; (3) processes: our culture tends to be impatient and we try to solve problems quickly, contrary to TQM's careful process analysis; and (4) professionalization: professional staff can be resistant to turning over their practices and services to what they perceive as the "uniformed whims of the customer".

Summary

Libraries are ideal places to implement TQM. They are service organizations dedicated to their customers, the patrons. By formulating a strategic plan, and following it with a commitment to continuous quality improvement, library managers can transform and improve their organizations. The notable principles of TQM are: (1) manage by fact: make library decisions after careful analysis of data gathered with tools such as checksheets, histograms, and Pareto charts; (2) eliminate rework: library work is often labour-intensive—simplify it and make sure it is done properly the first time; (3) respect people and ideas: staff are the library's most valuable resources, and they should be encouraged to point out problems without fear of management; and (4) empower people: trust library staff to act responsibly and give them the appropriate authority to make decisions that can improve the quality of work they do. Finally, remember that TQM is not a "quick fix". It needs to be implemented gradually over a two-to-three-year period.

NOTES

1. S. Shridharan and S. Kumar. "Total Quality Management in Libraries." XLL ILA Conference, Vijaywada; 1996; pp. 17-21.
2. K.C. Dabas and Sheela Dabas. "Impact of automation on library management techniques." In PSG Kumar & C.P. Vashishtha (Ed.). "Human Relations in Librarianship" Seminar Paper 41st; All India Library Conference. Vijaywada. ILA. Jan. 7-10, 1995; pp. 313-323.
3. K.C. Dabas and Sewa Singh. "Information Management in University Libraries: Reality and desirability in the new millennium." In Information Management in new millennium. SIS, INSA Conf. N. Delhi, 2000.
4. B.M. Meena. "Total Quality Management. Application to libraries and information centers: Basic Issues:" XVII. ILA Seminar. Dec. 10-13, 1996; pp. 155-160.
5. Thakur R. Sinha. "TQM in special libraries and Inf. Centres." IASLIC seminar. XVII, Calcutta, 1996; pp. 105-109.
6. S. Jurow and S.B. Bernard. "Integrating total quality management in library sitting". Binghamton: Howarth Press, 1993.
7. M. Wattan. "The Deming Management System", New York: Perijee, 1986.
8. A.F. Sirkin. "Customer service, Another side of TQM". *Journal of Library Administration*. 18-12; pp.71-83.

Resource Sharing

16

In 1986, a national policy on Library and Information System was formulated. It recommended that the national libraries should form an integrated system for a better Coordination of their activities and services. The Planning Commission had set up a working group on modernization of library and Information Service to share the resources for optimum utilization. The other effort was the UGC report on Information and library network (INFLIBNET) which proposed a mechanism to establish a network connecting universities, colleges, documentation centers, etc. through communication technology.

NISSAT (National Information Systems for Science and Technology) was the creation to coordinate with the sectoral information systems in the field of cooperation in resource sharing. NISCAIR is the national body to provide and promote information services nationally and internationally. Centralized acquisition of foreign periodicals (CAP), document delivery and compilation of union catalogue are the main contributions of NISCAIR towards resource sharing.

When two or more libraries and/or other organizations are engaged in a common pattern of information exchange, through communications there is a network. A network usually consists of a formal arrangement whereby materials, information and service provided by a variety of libraries and other organizations are available to all potential users.

Alphonse defines network as a formal organization among libraries for co-operation and sharing of resources, in which the group as a whole is organized into subgroups, with the exception that most of the needs of a library will be satisfied within the subgroups of which it is a member.

Library networks have following characteristics:

Data: Bibliographic records (MARC) frequently

Retrieval: Author/title (subject)
(Keyword/Terms)

Access: Telecommunication network/private network

Users: Librarians

Special features:

- one type of data
- committed user base
- high professional needs
- low end-user needs

16.1 Historical Development

Cooperation is a social activity as old as human civilization itself. The aim of any cooperative activity is to achieve what the members of the group can't achieve individually. The fascination for cooperative endeavour, later envolved into division of labour among individual members and subsequently to specialization.

16.1.1 Forms of resource sharing

Resource sharing is a need-based concept founded on sound principle of give and take. It is not the quantum of exchange but the real desire to do so that is essential to become part and parcel of the important programme of resource sharing. Among the resource-sharing activities, interlibrary loan, document delivery services and exchange of publications, hold an important place.

16.1.2 Goals

Resource sharing denotes a mode of operation, whereby functions are shared in common, by a number of libraries. According to Allen Kent, the goals are to provide a positive net effect: (a) on the library user, in terms of access to more materials or services; and /or (b) on the library budget, in terms of providing level service at less cost, increased service at level cost, or much more service at less cost, than if undertaken individually. These goals should be realized without harm to the missions of participating libraries, although their methods of operation invariably must be adjusted. Similarly, the goals are realizable, only with some changes in the habits of users.

16.2 Development

History of resource sharing can be traced to 200 BC, when Alexandria library shared its resources with Pergamon library. Among the later developments, the formal cooperative effort known as 'resource sharing' includes available resources, to respond to the reader's service at the libraries. Government agencies, professional organizations and individual institutions began to set standards and organize information networks. They found that certain functions, such as Cataloguing, could be done more efficiently in a central location, with the results distributed to participating institutions. They found that little used research material could be acquired and stored in a central place, and be distributed to interested scholars. The development of cooperative organization took an entirely new significance for libraries as the computer began to change the face of library operations. The first major cooperative effort in automation was within academic libraries.

The development of computer technology, coupled with an unabated increase in the cost of library materials, provided fertile ground for growth of resource sharing among American and European libraries, in the 20th century. The amount of resource sharing occurring among libraries took quantum leaps during the 1970s and 1980s, due to creation and widespread acceptance of computerized bibliographic networks. Important foundation had been laid during the late 1960s, with the creation of MARC Communication Format by the Library of Congress for machine readable cataloguing (MARC) and offering both the format and data from its own cataloguing operation, to any organization willing to experiment.

Another step was in the area of document delivery. For this purpose, idea of the telefacsimile (better known as fax) was introduced in the 19th century, in which a device was developed, which could send an electronic current over wires and reproduce the motion of a pendulum. In the middle of 1980's revised group III fax machines, capable of very fast transmitting, with a significant drop in the price of the equipment, resulted in almost overnight enthusiastic acceptance of fax. By 1989, 77% of all US business organizations had installed telefacsimile machines, while 50% of the government and education locations had access to fax equipment. The relatively low cost makes it a feasible equipment for libraries.

An early example of technology getting in the way of resource sharing, is the use of microform for back files of journals for space saving or security reasons. With microform there is more staff work required to produce the copy requested for interlibrary loan, reader printers are very costly and cost of each copy is very high. In more recent developments, it is not yet clear where 'hypermedia publications', containing sound, picture and text, as well as interactive sections, should fit into resource sharing. CD-ROM technology has the potential to effect and change dramatically resource sharing at the local, national and international levels. The positive aspect of automating collections are apparent with CD-ROM technology. Most notable is its large storage capacity. It is now an affordable method for providing library services, and has a low per copy replication cost, for additional workstation whether they are in house or in another library. CD-ROM can and does function as a back up catalogue, and the database, once built, can migrate to different technologies. The wide range of CD-ROM products and services involved, have made it difficult for librarians and libraries to analyse and focus on the implications of this impact on resource sharing. If CD-ROM technology is to be adopted and used by libraries in any semblance of a planned and organized fashion, then this impact must be recognized and anticipated by all libraries, from the school level to the largest research institution.

Electronic mail (E-mail) is the latest in the line of postal, telex and fax systems of communication. It is one of the important network based services, available to E-mail users for sending and receiving messages across the world. It is projected as the cheapest and fastest channel for disseminating information across the globe. Application of E-mail in information processing centers ensures fast and speedy transmission of information products. The main application of E-mail is rather in online information service, than in message handling. An E-mail user can avail online service, cutting across geographical barriers, irrespective of the distance, between user terminal and database host system. Other E-mail applications including computerized literature searches, reference enquiries, photocopies supply, interlibrary loan, reserves and renewals that have been offered in different libraries.

16.3 Resource Sharing Through Networks

Inflation and budget reductions are the primary forces that lead to resource sharing in libraries. Consortium, network and organizational arrangements are main concerns for achieving a variety of resource sharing objectives. Resource sharing requires access to circulation of information to avoid disappointment, and to accelerate the process of locating the required information at another library. If resource sharing is to be deemed successful, it must occur with the desired material in hand, well before need has evaporated.

Areas for Resource Sharing (Traditional)

Inter-Library Loan

Union Catalogues

Co-operative acquisition

Co-operative cataloguing

Resource sharing is necessary because of exponential information growth, increasing cost of information materials, technological advancements that offer newer methods of information processing, retrieval and dissemination. Increasing emphasis on avoidance of wastage due to unnecessary duplication of information sources.

Communication and Change

The new media of communication plays a very important role, not only in bringing the patron, the required information in a variety of new forms, but also in expediting inter-library coordination, by forging ever more strongly the bonds of cooperation that will eventually make available the total intellectual resources of a nation at any one point of need.

The combination of computer and communication technology applied to libraries, has expanded the horizons of the individual library. The computer networking has opened the possibility of sharing the bibliographic systems and the databases of libraries.

It has major impetus in library development in the following areas:

(b) Optimization of collection in libraries with limited budget.

(c) To promote and support adoption of standards in library operations.

(d) To improve efficiency of housekeeping operations.

(e) To generate new services and to improve the efficiency of the existing services.

Pre-requisites for Resource Sharing Network

(a) Agreements for implementing cooperation;

(b) Establishment of facilities for sharing little used materials;

(c) Agreements on acquisition policies to ensure consistent development of holdings to avoid redundancy.

(d) Methods of adequate delivery of resources to users (the output media).

(e) The subject interest area should be a common one among the centers being connected.

(f) Compatibility between the computing systems available with the organizations to be netted is essential.

(g) Adequate means of information dissemination.

(h) Formal established organizational cooperation.

(i) Established and functioning communication links (telephone, telex, fax, satellite communication channels).

16.4 Telecom & Software Standards

Technology is now—and will remain—both a force for progress and an obstacle to progress. Impressive advances in bibliographic resource sharing have been made because the power of technology was harnessed by the use of standards like MARC. The lack of standardization which remains in the world of telecommunications, applications software and Electronic Mail (E-mail), etc. will need to be addressed before the information society can become a reality. Technological advance will probably continue to outstrip the ability of the people to link the old and the new. The shift from print based materials to electronic materials, well present creating system for seamless electronic resource sharing.

16.5 Resource Sharing and Technology

There are various categories of informations which need different approaches and systems to be used. But there is a new outlook on the horizon and a climate in which an appreciable degree of interaction is beginning to take place between people working in different sectors.

The machines have taken over all the routines of selection, abstracting, indexing and cataloguing, previously done by professional information officers and libraries. The steadily growing range of commercially available, subject-oriented current awareness services in hard copy forms, devalued the importance of the inhouse bulletins. As the computer capabilities increased to use peripheral equipment made its appearance, online access to information that user needs will be only a telephone connection for information, to dial the appropriate file, from his terminal[1].

The library service of a great city can, and surely ought to be, something more than a couple of hundred accidental heaps of miscellaneous volumes, each maintained and managed in jealous isolation from the rest, and limited in its public utility by the lack of communication between the heaps—even, usually, by a dense ignorance in those in charge of each heap, as to what may be hidden in every other heap. Since the 20th century tremendous advances in technology, information and communication and production of information and knowledge and then came the developments in space and satellite technology and the advent of computers, which together brought about a change in the horizon of information, knowledge and libraries.

The flow of information from all sources would continue to increase, at an even faster rate than at present. Indications are that expenses associated with acquiring, processing, storing, and retrieving, will continue to increase at a faster rate than library budgets. To a large extent our culture is producing information much like one amoeba produces another. The great amount is not the direct result of users making specific inquiries. It is the result of parent concepts, generating off-spring, because there is an inevitability in the growth of knowledge. The impetus to produce more information, is more a factor of what has already been produced, than a user's demand for specific knowledge.

16.5.1 Networks

The evolution of simple inter-library book lending into the present complexities of library networking, depended initially, on the application of the telephone to the task of inter-library co-operation. The next step was the introduction of tele-type facilities known in the United Kingdom as TELEX. The first facility of this type, to be extensively published as a viable library information transmitting facility, was installed in the Commercial Library of the Manchester Public Libraries in the early 1950s. By the mid-1960s, telex-transmission had become a major feature of the formal inter-library cooperation system, for book and periodical loans, especially in respect of the activities of the National Leading Library for Science and Technology (now known as British Library Lending Division).

With the evolution of sophisticated computer technology computer has become the key component of a communication system, allowing almost limitless capacity for information transfer, and facsimile transmission of actual documents, between any two points, possessing relatively ordinary provisions, such as telephones, computer terminals, television screens and other ancillary equipment.[2]

There are three principal problems of co-operative computer networks, for reference service and library operations.

1. The library needs to standardize the range of bibliographic data stored in various library databases, so that each individual source is 'readable' with the help of networks, and readily adaptable to their particular needs.
2. The need to develop the ability to improve the speed of access to the documents that are readily visible to a literature search and the access to documents facilities, the breaking down of legal, political and cultural barriers, to the free availability of documents across national boundaries (copyright restrictions).
3. Financial constraints, retraining and reorganisation of existing staff and reformation of their attitudes towards the work, considering the efficiency of networking environments.

Advantages

(a) Provides greater magnitude of service;

(b) Extends the range of services and to improve service performance;

(c) To bring into focus new objectives not possible for the individual library, through library's acting in concert;[3]

(d) An awareness of the total library scene and of affinities between library services; and

(e) Professional ethics of service, over mere institutional loyalty.

Disadvantages

(a) Libraries vary in their stages of development and differ in what they demand from and to what extent they can participate in co-operative activity;

(b) Library policy and finance fall within the framework of a parent organization.

16.5.2 MARC

The development by LC and British Library Bibliographic Services Division of the MARC format was an important step in the evolution of networking capacity. Maurice Line describes the joint project mounted by UNESCO and IFLA under the title "Universal Availability of Publications" (UAP).

16.5.3 CATV

In the United States Cable Television (CATV) was used potentially in library operations. The first American Public Library to employ CATV was the Natrona Country Library in Wyoming, which began transmission in 1970.

16.5.4 Conferencing

The British General Post Office's CONFRAVISION service enables meetings and conferences to be held by groups of people sitting in their own offices in various parts of the country. Although, it is very expensive, it has brought massive and revolutionary changes that communication technology is bringing to all walks of life. The impending change was brought by the British Post Office's PRESTEL service, initially known as VIEWDATA. Cawkwell described PRESTEL system in a simple way.[4]

"The system's potential for storing and retrieving information is virtually limitless. To receive specific data the individual subscriber to the service, uses a small hand-held push-button device, not unlike a pocket calculator, which is linked to the telephone/television adaptation, and with it instructs the computer to display required data on the television screen".

The range of data through PRESTEL covers news services, weather reports, current affairs and consumer news, radio and TV programmes information, etc.

16.5.5 Resource sharing tools

The principal means used as vehicles of co-operation, themselves of the product of co-operative action are bibliographies, union catalogues, union lists, abstracts, indexes and directories. Bibliographies union list used in co-operation, merges into the wider field of bibliographical control. Abstracts and Indexes would appear to be an ideal field for collaboration 'with the idea of making sure that as much as possible is abstracted once, and nothing more than once' to prevent duplication of effort and omission. Directories serve a referral function to resources on national, regional, local and subject lines.

There are following bibliographical sources which cooperate in resource sharing[5]:

1. BLAISE: (British Library Automated Information Service). It serves current and retrospective online access to UK and LC MARC record. It was introduced in 1977.
2. BRS: (Bibliographic Retrieval Service). It serves to provide innovative and cost-effective online search service. Its major service provides online access to bibliographic and full-text databases. It also offers SDI service. It was introduced in 1976.
3. ESA-IRS: (The Information Retrieval Service of the European Space Agency (ESA) (Frascate Italy). It offers online search service in the early 1970s via a special telecommunication network ESANET. It provides access via online process to more than 25 databases, mainly on nuclear and space sciences on EURONET.
4. DIALOG: The DIALOG information retrieval service is sponsored by Lockheed Information Services at Palo Alto in California. It started in 1972. This search software was prepared from the RECON (Remote Console) developed by Lockheed for the National Aeronautics and Space Agency, USA. It comprises 192 databases, out of which majority are scientific and technical. It contains over 16 million bibliographic citations, available online, CAS and SDI services online.
5. OCLC: (Online College Library Center) (previously known as Ohio College Library Center), USA. It enables cataloguing and other bibliographic data to be swiftly and economically transmitted over long distances and across national and linguistic boundaries.

NOTES

1. Harrod's Librarians Glossary of terms used in librarianship. Documentation and the bookcrafts. Ed. 5. Revised and updated by Ray Pryth ench. Hunt, Gower, 1984; pp. 378-379.

2. T.S. Rajgopalan. "Trends and Perspectives in Indian Librarianship". ILA Conference. XXXIII. Trichirapalli, 1987; pp. 4-6.
3. UNESCO. UNESCO *Databases on CD-ROM*. 2nd ed.
4. Global Information Systems Technology Pvt. Ltd., New Delhi; Brochure, 1994; pp. 11-13.
5. K. Rajshekharan. "Computer aided information access agriculture". Computerisation and library network. Delhi: ALA, 1991; pp. 157-159.

Information Technology: A Revolution in Higher Education

17

Information Technology will change the world more permanently and more profoundly than any technology so far seen in history and will bring about a transformation of civilization to match.

Johi-Diebold

There is now broad consensus that IT is shaping our world. IT involves use of computers and information systems for storing, managing and accessing useful information in an optimized and organized way. Storage of a large volume of data, effective data management, maintenance of data management, maintenance of data consistency and integrity and quick and ready access of data are some of the major features of IT. Earlier computers belonged only to institutions and large organizations. Now the "personal" computers have placed computing power in the hands of numerous individuals. After the invention of the microprocessor, high density storage devices, video tape recorders, compact discs, optical cables, satellite telecommunications and other information and communication technologies appeared.

In India, significant developments in the use of computers have taken place in the industrial and commercial sectors. Computers have wide applications in educational sectors also. It is essential that the educational sector, specifically the higher education segment, adopts and integrates computers in its system to improve quality and productivity. According to the UNESCO report—Learning: the Treasure Within (1996), the functions of higher education are as follows: Universities should be central to the higher level of the system, to prepare students for research and teaching; to provide highly specialized training courses adapted to the needs of economic and social life; to be open to all so as to cater for the many aspects of life education in the widest sense; international cooperation.

The computer, with its versatility, accelerates one's ability to solve many problems related to teaching, research and administration that are encountered in higher education to achieve its goal.

After the National Policy on Education (1986) was formulated, quite a few reforms were introduced which have had a significant influence on the quality, quantity and equity in higher education. To improve the quality of higher education through orientation and reorientation of college teachers on a regular basis, a number of academic staff colleges were established. Efforts have been made to improve access to higher education in the rural areas by opening institutions in rural areas, promoting open and distant learning and the introduction of vocational courses at the college level. Realising the importance of technology in higher education, information technology has also been introduced in some institutions through computers, and other facilities for modernization and automation.

In fact, a decade ago whenever computers were introduced in any educational institution, its primary goal was to devise a variety of courses in computer competence. Then comes a secondary use of computers in research, administration and teaching. Thus, teaching about computers can be viewed in two phases: (1) Developing a pool of computer professionals, and (2) Developing a generation of computer users. There are many benefits of using information technology in teaching learning process at higher education.

(a) There are no longer geographical boundaries for learning any concept. Full independence is given to the learner to select desirable education.

(b) It promotes independent, flexible according to one's own level and pace, a type of learning where students take projects that relate to application of curriculum in practical aspect.

(c) It provides man with approaches through its hypermedia and multimedia characteristic. It allows an individual to use his/her multiple cognitive abilities to the fullest extent. It assures life-long learning.

A learner living anywhere in the world can pay fees through draft and get access to any course of interest through e-mail and internet. One can refer to library resource in virtual system. Virtual classrooms are soon becoming a reality. The students can chat among themselves and can also talk with the expert/ resource person through the network. The electronic mail is one of the boons of Information Technology. Networks may be set up to foster communication in the form of e-mail. It is possible to deliver message immediately using e-mail which is faster than conventional internal mail services.

IT has certain barriers to overcome. (1) It is concentrated in developed countries due to high cost of connections, low telephone and computer line ratio, lack of electricity; (2) Cost of network, access, lack of system support to fast and slow learners; (3) Educational sites on the Internet require more structuring and systematization for someone to learn a body of knowledge; (4) There is a great deal of information and instruction on the web in false, dangerous and of poor quality; (5) High level of illiteracy and lack of computer skills are obstacles to effective use and access to ICTs; and (6) the cyberspace is rapidly becoming an electronic mall whose main activity is electronic or e-commerce rather than public debate and education.

The number of institutions where computers are used as a teaching aid is insignificant. As the institutions are not using computers for pedagogy the research carried out in the use of computer in pedagogy is also significant. The reason for this low use may be due to lack of technical support to the faculty for developing computer aided material and availability of relevant hardware and software. In India, there is a lack of empirical studies of computers, some research studies have been carried out in different disciplines at various centers of national importance such as National Center for Software Technology (NCST), Tata Institute of Fundamental Research (TIFR), etc.

Efforts have been made in teaching languages, computer courses, mathematics and science.

There are certain competencies required in order to use IT. One must know self managed learning, scientific and technological terms, information handling, selection, retrieval and critical assessment of information, systems thinking and system design, inquiry exploration and experimentation. Technology is only a tool which has to be mastered, one should not be mastered by it. Because technological revolution is dismantling borders, teachers cannot afford to be left out. With the use of IT a person should not become isolated. Therefore other competencies like, collaborative work, team work, use and management of multiple resources, flexible use of technologies is required as also job market orientation.

Building the human infrastructure is a gradual process that should be designed and developed as a key component. It requires a strong pedagogical support system to support teachers in various ways. That would need well conceived plans at the apex level of higher education to ensure uniform quality standards. After all, we should not forget the fact that our success in this century will largely depend on our progress in the field of IT. This is the major responsibility of our universities. There is a broad consensus that IT is shaping our world.

17.1 Information Technology and its Impact

Changing Scenario in the Contemporary Society

In earlier times, education was for acquiring knowledge rather than for employment, but in the post-industrial society it has become a major prerequisite for employment. Telecommunication and computer technology have merged to form the new field called information technology. As technology changes, necessary skills change. Even if education is seen from a purely vocational point of view—as providing skills relevant to work—lifelong exposure to education will be needed in the future.

IT is emerging as a major driving force for global economy. It is going to be the vehicle of technological revolution in every field. The changes are partly the result of financial constraints faced by higher education section and partly due to the advances in IT and communications.

17.1.1 Online education

The merging of IT and education has emerged as online education, which could be:

- From teaching to learning.
- From on campus "Classroom" education to home, work place and community based education.
- From single institution to consortia of institutions networked together by electronic communication.
- From traditional students to non-traditional students.

There are many existing sites on online learning and many companies have started investing heavily in web education.

Heading towards the same goal, online varsity which is launched by Aptech Limited combines the features of real life classroom learning with the flexibility and power of the internet. One can chat and discuss online with experienced online tutors and with fellow students. It also offers powerful learning support features such as online counseling, tutoring, library, bulletin board, etc.

Distance Learning in the US delivers approximately 90,000 courses at college and universities. Among the current and prospective operators of virtual classroom are, the established universities that want to expand their reach without expanding their physical plants. In the same direction India has offered IGNOU online Management Course, as a part of its Management Education through Interactive Delivery Systems (MEIDS) project. The project will function in association with 20 management institutes in various parts of the country. These Institutes will be partners in advanced learning systems (PALS) where the students will get enrolled online, submit assignment using client-server technology and access the digital library and other referral material on the net.

E-Book

18

There have been many significant technological advances during the last two decades but until the advent of the Internet and electronic commerce, the book industry remained essentially unchanged. Even today, publishers produce printed books and sell them through bookstores. It is currently estimated that approximately 100,000 new book titles per year are published, and that the book publishing industry generates over $90 billion in revenues annually. Despite the attractive qualities of printed books, they are extremely costly to produce, store, ship, and sell. Because they are a static medium, revisions typically take a significant amount of time and effort to produce, so there is often little incentive to keep them upto date. The success of the retrieval is generally only as good as the indexing. Distributing books electronically has therefore been a continuing gleam in the eyes of developers of electronic information products. The most recent trend in the book industry is the development of electronic books (or E-Books).

18.1 What are E-Books

A text or monograph which is available in an electronic format. E-Books are simply digital versions of books that can be obtained electronically and stored and read on either a traditional personal computer, a common handheld device or a dedicated E-Book 'reader'.

It is needed because:

(a) Its ability to store a number of books at one time is really great.

(b) Because E-Books are basically text-based files, we can search for a certain part of an E-Book without having to flip through it endlessly.

(c) It is difficult to carry a large number of E-Books on Pocket PC at one time, the Pocket PC is not only smaller than a paperback book, it also performs all of those other functions that Pocket PC excels at.

(d) The contents of a book are available on a website for downloading to the user's PC.

(e) The book's contents are downloaded to a dedicated hardware device which has a high-quality screen and special capabilities for book reading.

(f) The E-Book remains on the provider's website and can be accessed for free. Readers can 'purchase' the books to receive indefinite access.

(g) The contents of a book are stored in a system connected to a high-speed, high-quality printer, from which printed and bound copies are produced on demand and can be available on a chapter-by-chapter basis to enable the creation of single copies of customized books.

18.2 Buying and Storing E-Books

(a) *Via a PC*

(i) Visit an online bookshop, purchase book as usual.

(ii) Book available for immediate download to a PC.

(iii) Downloaded to E-Book reader from PC.

(b) *Via E-Book reader*

(i) Plug reader directly into a phone socket and manage the process via the reader itself.

(ii) Copies of books held on PC hard disk.

(iii) Book vendor creates personalized online bookshelf on your behalf.

(iv) Books copied to reader when required.

(c) Each E-Book being encrypted can only be unencrypted by the reader for which it was purchased with systems of passwords.

Why Beneficial

(i) They're quicker to obtain.

(ii) E-Books are more updated and upgraded.

(iii) Usually one gets far more than just the book.

(iv) E-Books take up less space.

(v) E-Books don't use up trees: E-Books use very few natural resources also.

(vi) They're more portable: Quick and easy access to hundreds of books on your desktop computer, notebook or E-Book reader is possible.

(vii) Easy links to websites and other references can be placed in an electronic book. While reading, we can click on hot links to other places to find out more.

(viii) E-Books can be branded with one's name and one can allow others to brand one's E-Books with their name.

(ix) Global searches and ability to find information quickly: It saves the time.

(x) This is an emerging technology and people are often slow to change.

Limitations

(i) Require equipment to be read.

(ii) Not as accessible as print based books.

(iii) Unfamiliar and new.

(iv) Low market penetration.

(v) Different standards currently in use.

(vi) Lower sales.

Format: E-publishing initially required readers to have certain software for E-Books. Most of them have now adapted their formats to serve their customers better. E-Books are now available in a variety of forms like 'pdf' for Adobe Acrobat, text formats, HTML and disks for Windows. Keep in mind that not everyone has the latest technology. Mac users often encounter compatibility problems as well.

E-Book Challenge

(a) Libraries circulate E-Book readers with a number of titles pre-loaded.

(b) E-Books have records included in the catalogue.

(c) The only E-Books available are those installed on the circulating E-Books readers.

(d) Limited choice for users, online users unable to read library's E-Books on their own e-book readers.

(e) Can be downloaded directly from the library catalogue to user's preferred E-Book reader.

(f) Only one user, at one time to each purchased copy of the E-Book.

(g) Books removed automatically from user's E-Book reader at the end of loan period and made instantaneously available in the catalogue again.

(h) Existing book suppliers expand to include E-books.

(i) New organizations manage E-book access and acquisition on behalf of the library.

(j) Access through passwords and authentication procedures.

(k) Internet accessible micro payments—per page view.

An Intranet is a network built inside institutions that uses ICT technologies to enable the usage/sharing of documents and collation of data using web pages. The Intranet system integrates organisation's structure so as to become the primary path for learners to obtain work-related documents, share knowledge, collaborate on designs, and access for mining the data. An Intranet system has, usually, access to Intranet by which it can communicate independent of topographical location.

It leads to efficiency in administration, teaching, learning, and internal communications and has a good, updated useful content for easy access to the users.

Exponential growth of Internet is greatly contributing to the ICT revolution. With Internet becoming pervasive, organizations/ institutions realized the advantages in (1) integrating their internal information networks with Internet, and (2) applying the same technologies for internal/external purposes. It is defined as networks centers around the web technologies for in-house information flow. Intranet is the application of network computing in general, within an organization to facilitate the internal flow of information.

Internet is having a profound effect on how we communicate. The Intranet ensures access of inhouse information with security. Both large and small institutions/organizations have implemented this technology, improving efficiency at reducing costs.

The IT revolution that we are witnessing today has the power to unleash unimaginable opportunities to provide better quality with good services and efficient delivery system. Decisions in today's global information age need to be made instantly. Lack of time to browse through innumerable number of pages of printed material to find a piece of information is a key factor for Intranet. Some of the costs of adage transaction include:

(a) Huge printing and distribution costs associated with documents that are rarely used.
(b) Lack of access to vital information delays in reaching clientele needs.
(c) Outdated information leads to poor decisions based on erroneous assumptions.
(d) The trapping of information in proprietary computer systems requires costly updating of desktop interfaces every time.
(e) Dissimilar file formats and operating systems mean certain departments just cannot exchange information digitally, forcing them to resort to costly paper-based methods.

However, Intranet is an organization-wide information distribution system that uses Internet tools and technology. It is a smaller version of the Internet that only the members of an organization can have access and use. Organisations can create manageable, secured version of the World Wide Web so as to facilitate better knowledge flow for effective collaboration.

18.3 Quality of Intranet

(a) *Reduction in paper*: Organisations can process their documents for decisions online reducing time consumption and paperwork.

(b) *Client interface*: The web browser can become a universal interface to the systems and information, resulting in low cost of ownership of the desktop as the browser can serve as the interface to many different data sets.

(c) *Easy usage*: If the people know how to use a mouse then they will be able to learn how to point and click through the web of hyper-linked documents on the Intranet.

(d) *Connects across disparate platforms*: Organisations with reticulated usage of UNIX, MAC can reach end user. It can rapidly browse and mine the data using HTML text.

(e) *Open architecture*: Internet protocols are open as per standards set by global governing bodies. This gives the power to retrieve the data from the archival databases.

(f) *Self-service*: With one click, one can directly access the solution to the problem. One is able to choose the time to access information making them more time-efficient.

(g) *Dynamic information*: Documents that are on paper are now placed on the internal web. These web documents can be updated more often and with greater ease than their paper counterparts with precision for policy/decision.

(h) *Global access*: Knowledge stored on the Intranet can be accessed from any TCP/IP network in the world as long as the user is authorized to connect through Intranet.

(i) *Richness of multimedia*: Intranets can publish text, graphics and animation but also have the power to publish audio and video in webgogy mode.

(j) *Work culture*: An Intranet can build a new culture for rapid processing of information within the organization like collect, collate and build data based upon information exchange and collaboration.

18.4 Prerequisites

Intranet is not specifically a tool, it is rather a vehicle supporting the system in carrying out the assigned tasks at a rapid pace. The introduction of Intranet requires a mindset/cultural change within the organisation/institution to adapt the system. Intranet is a state-of-the-art facility, viz. computers connected via a LAN or WAN and other network peripherals. Many institutions usually possess most of the gadgets of the state-of-the-art facility but for requirements of few peripherals. Most of the Intranet software is either freeware/shareware or available at a subsidized price for educational institutions.

18.5 Components

(a) The *web software* server stores documents, sends back files or executes programs. The work is stored on a web server that enables users to search stored documents information whose author is known.

(b) The *hypertext markup language* (HTML) code, the language of the web used to format text and set up links.

(c) *A graphic editor* manipulates images and saves them into proper file formats supported by most web browsers.

(d) An animation tool for producing video special effects.

(e) A search engine to find information and documents on the web.

18.6 Governance of the Intranet

(a) *Content*: The institution needs to facilitate the data as primary content of the Intranet material and keep updating it.

(b) *Ensuring the Intranet is used*: Learners need to be sensitized for usage of Intranet for all means of information and communication.

(c) *Continuous review*: As the Intranet grows in size and scope, it needs to be kept under continuous review to ensure its accessibility, for its precise content.

(d) *Ongoing management of the Intranet*: Institutions need to hire technical expertise for updation of website, database / management, and back end server programming with continuous review of the web content.

(e) *Lack of inter-operability*: Since next-generation systems cannot "talk to each other", they automatically become less useful.

(f) *Lack of security*: Lack of security is perhaps the key concern slowing the development of Intranets. However, rapid developments in secure transactions technology, certification, and encryption are making this concern less important. A key feature of new Cyber law will allow security through a system of cryptography.

(g) *Lack of legal and regulatory systems*: The next-generation Intranet technologies are evolving much more quickly than the social framework needed to support them, viz. the digital signatures.

(h) *Lack of uniform access*: Some institutions and individuals do not have access to computers or data communications networks like the Internet, impeding use of web applications for electronic governance. Alternative channels of distribution will have to exist beside electronic media.

Therefore, Intranet is rapidly approaching a more mature and complex stage. In the future, the Internet, Intranet and Extranet will become even more integrated into institution/organizational needs with an integrated services.

18.7 Is Internet a Substitute

Librarians need to play a renewed role in this digital world. This most profound technological development—a connection of computer to computer in an unbroken chain around the world—may alter the fundamental concept of the library in the twenty-first century. But this technology will not substantially alter the business of librarians—connecting people with information. Sometimes the library and information science professionals, start feeling that libraries are really in trouble, grave danger when important higher education officials say

'Internet has made libraries obsolete'. But the same is not true as reading 'is culture'. Internet is a substitute of the library.

18.8 Why Substitute

(a) Finding information on the web is like finding a shell in an ocean. The quality of information is quite variable. Internet, in fact, is the place to find an answer in three days for a query that would take three hours in a library. Irrespective of the searcher meta search engines (Lycos, Alt Vista, Google, etc.) one finds as if Internet is a vast uncatalogued library. The basic problem in finding information on Internet is that even if one knows the exact URL and has it book marked or written down, there is no guarantee it will work next year, or even next week.

(b) It is estimated that over one billion web pages are available on the Internet. But out of these many pages very few are free of cost.

(c) One of the problems with Internet is that when one wants to have access to articles, one finds sites or footnotes or any other thing of the site often missing. Not only this but tables, graphs and formulae do not often show up in a reasonable way. Journal titles in digitized package change regularly without warning or prior notification. Sometimes one may find that page is not accessible as it has been moved from one place to another without giving new site location.

(d) Web is a collection of documents contributed from any authors and publishers who buy a web server. There is no quality control over the web and there is not likely to be any. Anyone can put up anything on the web. Thus, finding out what you want to know needs selection and filteration, but in finding what one wants to know in a sea of potentially interesting data, then turning it into useful information, perhaps needs extraordinary wisdom. The major reason for having too much irrelevant materials on the web is that web does not have a selection policy such as libraries where conscious efforts are made about what works will be acquired and maintained in the collection. In contrast to libraries' clearly defined development policies, the web looks more like the result of fantastically successful gifts programme: it includes the good, the bad, and the ugly.

(e) Users on the Net can easily and freely trade files regardless of any such protection. Thus, Internet information must provide for confidential, automated rights and royalty exchange ensuring users and owners that information is protected from unauthorized, accidental, or intentional misattribution, alteration, or misuse.

(f) Electronic information is still accessible only to a privileged few. Access requires equipment, connection costs, and also training for accessing digital information. The cost of access is going to remain high and for the vast majority of the world's population in developing countries having widespread Internet access, may be the equivalent of walking on the moon. Furthermore, the connections that do exist for more people are slow. In contrast, public libraries, even today, are the information reference points serving the least privileged in society.

(g) Librarians organize knowledge through the processes of subject analysis and cataloguing—creating information about information, or what is known as 'metadata'. On Internet there is need to develop methods of consistently and uniquely identifying and retrieving networked information, no matter what format they are or where they reside. Metadata standards are still in their infancy. Initiatives and research such as the Dublin Core/Warwick Framework for metadata, Government Information Locator Services (GILS), and Uniform Resource Characteristics (URC) are promising ways forward. But still a solution to the global resource discovery problem remains distant.

(h) The volume of information available on Internet is becoming a problem. We find the screen version of a valued publication much less user-friendly than its print equivalent or we cannot afford search time spent at a terminal to reach the page that used to arrive automatically in an in-tray. And then there is so much information available online that it is often difficult to rate it in terms of relevance and quality.

(i) We know very little about the sources of its materials, the type of documents available, the authoritativeness of the documents, the languages in which information is available, the age or longevity of the documents, the scope of subjects available, and other descriptive characteristics of an information collection.

(j) Electronic text is subtly different from print. An electronic mail message differs from a letter or office memorandum. There is no concept of leisure reading in digital environment as we can have in print media. We can borrow a book from a library and can read it at our leisure time over a cup of coffee which is not otherwise possible.

18.9 Conclusion

Thus it is clear that fraud, junk mailings, invasion of privacy, terrorism, pornography, sabotage are some of the issues related to Internet and they are going to cause troubles over the next few years. Since Internet is an international network, it has to merge the social norms and legal structures of every country in the world. Locating information on the Internet still remains highly inefficient as compared to traditional library sources, especially for unfamiliar users. The development of an infrastructure for the networked resource discovery and retrieval of highly distributed, autonomously created, and diverse electronic information is required.

Public libraries guard against the tyrannies of ignorance and conformity. Through their outreach programmes, libraries teach citizenship and develop multilingual and multicultural materials for their patrons. Librarians also become experts at helping others navigate the Internet. Similarly, libraries can create a physical reaction, a feeling of peace, respect, humility and honour that throws the mind wide open and suffuses the body with a near-spiritual pleasure. Libraries preserve records, a nation, a culture, a community and enable us to communicate through distance and time with the living and the dead. All this is made possible by library work of sorting, storing, indexing and preservation a work that will carry, in the electronic environment also.

18.9.1 E-Learning

With the emergence of World Wide Web (WWW) in 1969, the world of teaching and learning has adopted it as one of its main innovations. However, in spite of extensive use of the web in education, varieties of terminologies are used to depict this new field of knowledge.

18.9.2 Web with different terms

(a) *Web-based Instruction*: It is a 'hypermedia based instructional programme which utilizes the attributes and resources of the World Wide Web to create a meaningful learning environment where learning is fostered and supported".[1]

(b) *Virtual Learning*: "The educational process of learning over the Internet without having face-to-face contact is known as virtual learning.[2]

(c) *Online Lerning*: It is synonymous to web-based learning where learning is fostered via the WWW only, in an Intranet or Internet.[3] It is the new generation in the evolutionary growth of open, flexible and distance learning.

(d) *E-Learning*: The term e-learning covers a wide set of applications and processes including computer-based learning, web-based learning, virtual classroom, and digital collaboration.[4]

18.9.3 Some of the benefits of e-learning

(a) Access to educational resources from outside the institution on a global and instant basis;

(b) Quick and easy way to create, update and revise course materials through low-cost off-the-shelf software;

(c) Increased and flexible interaction with student through e-mail and discussion forums;

(d) Location and time independent delivery of course materials such as course notes, diagrams, reading list, etc.;

(e) Ability to combine text, graphics and a limited amount of multimedia, enabling instructional designers to prepare quality learning materials;

(f) Interactive and dynamic learning experience through online assessment tools, simulations and animated learning objects;

(g) Platform independent delivery, accessible through any computer with a simple browser interface;

(h) Increased learner control through hypertext based presentation of information;

18.9.4 Use of e-learning

(a) Web integrated in the classroom teaching, that works as supplement to the face-to-face teaching;

(b) Web used as a 'mixed mode' approach to complement face-to-face teaching, normally called 'blended e-learning'; and

(c) Web used independently for teaching and learning as replacement for face-to-face teaching.

18.9.5 Indian scene

The Government of India has always considered the use of Information and Communication Technologies (ICTs) as means of mass education. From the use of satellite in the early 1970s to the present interest in a dedicated satellite for education (EDUSAT), India has considered education as a primary force for development of the nation. India has a strong educational infrastructure, particularly in the higher education with 14,500 colleges and more than 260 universities. The developments related to e-learning should be seen in the context of socio-economic and ICT infrastructure of the country.[5] In spite of its low PC penetration and Internet access, India has progressed well in the IT sector primarily due to the IT training by the private sector. The country's first online educational enterprise also came with the private initiative, when the National Institute of Information Technology (NIIT Limited) started Netvarsity in 1996. Since then a large number of online 'teaching shops' are in operation primarily in the field of supporting school level education and for preparing students for competitive examinations like the medical and engineering entrance tests. However, National Association of Software and Services Companies (NASSCOM)'s Market Intelligence Service reports that the e-learning market in India is in an infant stage.

18.9.6 Developments[6]

Population:	1056.89 million
Population density:	334 per km
Per capita (US$) in 2002:	494
Main telephone lines:	48917000
Main telephone lines per 100 inhabitants:	4.63
Cellular mobile subscribers:	26154400
Cellular mobile subscriber per 100 inhabitants:	0.72
Total Internet hosts:	86871
Internet hosts per 10,000 inhabitants:	0.82
Total Internet users:	18481000
Internet users per 10,000 inhabitants:	174.86
Network Readiness Index Rank:	45

18.9.7 E-learning developments

The real impetus for e-learning came from the National Task Force on Information Technology and Software Development constituted by the Prime Minister of India in

1998. The Task Force report presents the master plan that India has in place as a long-term policy for capacity building of institutions, human resource development in IT related areas, and use of ICTs in education.[7]

18.9.8 NIIT and Netvarsity

The first online learning facility was established in 1996 by the NIIT. It became a separate subsidiary as NIIT Online Learning Limited (NOLL) in April 2000. It had more than 100,000 students enrolled for different courses. Though Netvarsity started as a fully online venture, at present it adopts a fusion mode where all the students of NIIT are automatically enrolled for Netvarsity and are required to complete 20 hours of the course each semester on the Internet. The courses of Netvarsity are mostly based on the "Skillette" concept, which is a short module of not more than 30 minutes that covers one specific unit of learning.[8]

18.9.9 Other organisations

(a) *IGNOU*—The IGNOU based VCI in 1999 with two programmes on information technology—the Bachelor of Information Technology (BIT) and Advanced Diploma in Information Technology (ADIT)—in collaboration with Edexcel, UK and the Government of India, Ministry of Information Technology, respectively. The VCI, apart from the web delivery of content, uses (i) live-satellite based teleconference lectures; (ii) recorded lectures; (iii) recorded video lectures; (iv) practical laboratories; (v) computer-based training tutorials; and (vi) online interactive chart.[9]

(b) *SSS*—The School of Social Sciences started the Post Graduate Certificate in Participatory Management of Displacement, Resettlement and Rehabilitation in 2001 with the support of the World Bank as a fully online programme. Other programme features include web course units with interactive exercises, online computer marked assignments, online diary submissions, e-counselling (chat) and e-library.[10]

(c) *Y.C.M. Open University*—YCMOU uses e-learning as a learner support mechanism especially for its Electronics Engineering Diploma Programme (EEDP). Students use a discussion forum to discuss concepts and clarify doubts. It was surveyed that online learning may be more effective by providing: (i) more 'expert' counselors who will respond quickly to student queries; (ii) more detailed information on the website; and (iii) more support from the coordinators as the study centre.[11]

Institution Applying E-learning

Sl. No	Name and URL	Areas Covered	Owned and Managed by
1.	Netvarsity http://www.netvarsity.com	IT related areas and soft skills	NIIT Online Learning Limited.
2.	Indira Gandhi National Open University http://www.ignou.ac.in	IT related areas and in Social Sciences	Part of the National Open University established by the Govt. of India.
3.	Yashwantrao Chavan Maharashtra Open University http://www.ycmou.com	Use e-learning as part of its distance learning strategy in technology courses	Part of YCMOU established by the Maharashtra State Government.
4.	Punjab Technical Univ. http://www.ptuonline.com	Engineering and Technology related courses	Established by the Govt. of Punjab, the online venture is a collaborative effort with a trust.
5.	Birla Institute of Technology & Sciences http://vu.bits-pilani.ac.in	Engineering courses	Part of the BITS (Deemed Univ. status accorded by the UGC).
6.	Institute of Management Technology http://www.imtonline.org	Courses in Mgmt. leading in e-MBA	Managed by NPO, and the courses approved by AICTE.
7.	Symbiosis Centre for Distance Learning http:/www.scald.net	Courses in Mgmt. leading to PG Diploma	Managed by Symbiosis Society (NPO) and approved by AICTE.
8.	MedVarsity http://www.medvarsity.com	Continuing education programmes in Medical and Health related topics	Management by Medvarsity Online Limited, a unit of Apollo Hospitals.

Sl. No	Name and URL	Areas Covered	Owned and Managed by
9.	Indian Institute of Technology, Mumbai http://www.dep.iitb.ac.in	IT related courses at diploma and non-credit level	Institute of National importance, and the programmes are offered by the Kanwal Rekhi School of I.T.
10.	Indian Institute of Technology, Delhi http:/www.iitd.ac.in/courses	Engineering course	Ministry of Information Technology, Govt. of India supported courses.

The Indian Institute of Management, Bangalore (IIMB) has been using e-learning to supplement face-to-face teaching. It experimented with online distance learning for short-term courses using the e-College Learning Management System.

Realizing the importance of the web-technologies, the University Grants Commission (UGC) organized a dialogue on "Enhancing Higher Education through E-Learning" in collaboration with the Commonwealth of Learning (COL), Vancouver from 17-19 November 2003 at New Delhi. The group recommended the following:[12]

1. UGC should create a system to support the use of e-learning by all institutions of higher learning in India, in an ambitious timeframe. Specifically the system should be learner-centred, cost-effective, affordable, inclusive, widely and easily accessible, scalable and up-gradable.
2. The goals of the system should be to:
   - (i) Enhance the quality of higher education through e-learning.
   - (ii) Change the teaching-learning paradigm.
   - (iii) Increase access with equity for higher education.
   - (iv) Make education relevant to sustainable human development.
3. The strategic plan for the initiative include:
   - (i) Policy guidelines on e-learning taking into account the goals of e-learning and bridging the digital divide.

(ii) Development of national infrastructure for e-learning, taking into account the present higher education infrastructure.

(iii) Recognition and reward for institutions and faculty for development and use of e-learning.

4. The implementation plan includes:

(i) The stages in the development of e-learning materials to be identified for design, production, delivery, evaluation and revision.

(ii) Setting up national standard for e-learning materials.

(iii) Initiation of pilot projects in the areas of job creation, income generation and socially relevant issues such as environment education.

The areas of e-learning:

(a) *Standard and Specifications*: To review standards including instructional design, learning object metadata, object packaging and digital rights management.

(b) *Hardware and Software*: To analyze the hardware and software requirements including learning management systems.

(c) *Connectivity*: To review and analyze the connectivity options including bandwidth available to the institutions.

(d) *User Studies*: To analyze the needs of learners and target groups and help in design of a client-centred system.

(e) *Content Related Issues*: To develop strategies in development of e-content and integrate them to classroom teaching.

(f) *Private Public Partnership*: To look into possible areas of collaboration amongst all stakeholders.

18.9.10 E-learning strategies

The development of e-learning in India is in its infancy, and the discussions and establishment of policy guidelines by the UGC would go a long way. There are many drawbacks in introducing the ICT in academic set-up:

Teachers have to make a move to new education, but lack time. Teachers fear that ICT will dislocate them. Teachers are unsure of the security provisions for their study materials, and perceived unreliability of networked services and local computing services.

It is important to develop teacher competencies in use of web-technologies, especially the use of e-learning platforms that are considered as empowering tools for teachers. There is a need for capacity building and training say "it needs to be understood that any new technology comes not merely with hardware and software, but with a learning and teaching style and grammar of its own, and that management practices need to be adapted in order to use the technologies effectively. However, we do not see any strategic effort in this direction, except for some sporadic training programmes conducted by organizations like IGNOU and the COL's regional center at New Delhi—The Commonwealth Educational Media Centre for Asia (CEMCA).

NOTES

1. B.H. Khan. *Web based instructions. What it is?* Eaglewood-Cliff: Edu. Tech. Pub., 1997, pp. 5-18.
2. D. French. "Internet based learning: An introduction and framework of Higher Edu. and business." London: Kagan Paul, 1999.
3. S. Misra. "Designing online learning." Vancouver: COL, 2001; pp. 5, 19.
4. Z. Berg and N. Collen. "Design guidelines for web based courses." Herqly: Idea group, 2000; pp. 3-40.
5. WEF (2003). "The Global Information Technology Report 2003-2004."
6. Source: http:/www.itu.int/ITUD/statistics
7. "India Govt. National task force on information technology and software development", N. Delhi: GOI, 1999.
8. S. Mitra. "Virtual institutions in the Indian subcontinent". Vancouver: The Commonwealth of learning, 2003; pp. 5, 19.
9. R. Sharma. "On-line delivery of programme." A case study of IGNOU, New Delhi: 2001.
10. S. Misra and S. Jain. "Design on on-line learning environment" ...Rehabititation Paper, Durban: Commonwealth July-Aug. 2003.
11. A. Deshmukh. "Student perceptions regarding on-line teaching and learning." Hong Kong: University, 2002, pp. 66-80.

12. UGC. Report of the dialogue on 'Enhancing higher education through e-Learning,' Nov. 17-19, 2003. India International Centre, New Delhi.